Relate is here for people who want to make their family relationships better.

We help people make sense of what's happening in their relationships, decide what they want to do and make those changes.

In addition to our respected and popular range of books, we have many other ways to support people. Our counsellors are trained professionals, and you can have a local appointment with one face-to-face or on the phone, or consult them online through our website. We also run relationship workshops.

We work with couples, families and individuals. Our network reaches across the whole of the UK, where we are the largest provider of relationship support and sex therapy.

Find more relationship advice and information about our services on our website at www.relate.org.uk or call us on 0300 100 1234.

Paula Hall is an Accredited Sexual and Relationship Psychotherapist, experienced in working with couples, families, individuals and young people, and has been a Relate counsellor for over 15 years. She currently works for Relate as a young people's and family counsellor and also works in private practice. She provides regular professional comment on divorce, separation and young people's issues to the national press, women's magazines, teenage magazines, websites, national and local radio and television, and runs her own website: www.TheRelationshipSpecialists.com

How to Have a Healthy Divorce

A step-by-step practical guide for anyone going through a separation or divorce

Paula Hall

relate

Vermilion
LONDON

1 3 5 7 9 10 8 6 4 2

Published in 2008 by Vermilion, an imprint of Ebury Publishing

Ebury Publishing is a Random House Group company

The Random House Group Limited Reg. No. 954009

Addresses for companies within the Random House Group can be
found at: www.rbooks.co.uk

A CIP catalogue record for this book is available
from the British Library

The Random House Group Limited supports The Forest
Stewardship Council (FSC), the leading international forest
certification organisation. All our titles that are printed on
Greenpeace approved FSC certified paper carry the FSC logo. Our
paper procurement policy can be found at
www.rbooks.co.uk/environment

Mixed Sources
Product group from well-managed
forests and other controlled sources
www.fsc.org   Cert no. TT-COC-2139
© 1996 Forest Stewardship Council

Printed and bound in Great Britain by
CPI Mackays, Chatham, ME5 8TD

ISBN 9780091924003

Copies are available at special rates for bulk orders. Contact the sales
development team on 020 7840 8487 for more information.

To buy books by your favourite authors and register for offers, visit
www.rbooks.co.uk

Contents

Introduction

A healthy divorce may seem like a complete contradiction to some, but why should that be so when we all know that happy endings are possible? A healthy divorce won't necessarily be pain-free or devoid of any stress or personal hardship, but then neither is a healthy eating plan or fitness regime. With perseverance, dedication and commitment, a healthy attitude can reap life-long benefits.

During the 15 years I've worked for Relate I've seen many divorcees – before, during and after the process. I can bear witness to the fact that although a healthy divorce is difficult, it is possible. Whether you separated from your ex five years ago or five minutes ago, it is your choice how you face your future. You can feel broken, empty, anxious and resentful for the rest of your life or you can choose to overcome the wounds of divorce and become happy and whole again. If your partner left you suddenly after many years together then your road to recovery may be longer, steeper and rockier than for someone who decides to end their marriage after a few unhappy years. But you can both choose the same goals and head in the same direction, even though your starting points are very different.

Divorce is a harsh reality in twenty-first century Britain and one that many feel powerless to avoid. Contrary to some cynical social commentators, I believe that the vast majority of people work hard to save their ailing marriages. They don't give up on a whim, seeing divorce as the easy option. But we're human, and humans make mistakes and get things wrong, and consequently relationships will fail. Years ago, people may have stayed together 'till death us do part', even if their marriage died many years before. They stayed in their unhappy marriages because that's what people did back then. Now, however, the option of divorce gives those trapped in unhappy marriages a second chance.

But what of those who are left – the people who thought they were in a happy marriage only to have it shattered by an emotionally meandering spouse? If this describes you, then divorce was not a positive choice, a purposeful decision that you made to improve your future. Nonetheless, it is your choice how you manage this devastating period in your life and the attitude you adopt for your future.

Having a healthy divorce is difficult because our emotions often tell us to behave in ways that are detrimental to our wellbeing. Grief can overwhelm us and make us feel powerless to do anything. Anger tells us to attack and pushes people away. Fear won't let us take risks in case we get hurt again, and the lies of guilt and rejection tell us we don't deserve to feel any better than this. But over the course of reading this book you will discover how to conquer those negative emotions and how to retrain your mind to think positively about yourself and your future.

First and foremost, *How to Have a Healthy Divorce* is a practical book. Throughout the pages you'll be encouraged to stop and take time to complete some simple exercises. These have been designed to help you personalise what you're reading so you may find it useful to have a notebook to hand as you read through each step. Step One explores how you can accept the reality of your new single status, whether you like it or not, and Step Two shows how the difficult emotions of grief, fear, anger, doubt and regret can be managed more effectively. Step Three will help you to develop strategies for personal growth and support; Step Four will explore friends, family and other support networks; and Step Five looks at how you can deal effectively with money and other practical matters. Step Six covers the essential art of communicating with your ex and co-parenting; and Step Seven gives you an opportunity to consider your dreams and ambitions for the future.

This is a challenging book. It doesn't pretend that divorce is easy or that following seven simple steps will get you to Nirvana. But it will show you that divorce is a turning point in your life, a time when you can take stock of everything that's been and decide where you want to go next. I know it's a horrible cliché, but divorce really is a 'learning opportunity', and you have the power to use your new-found education to make your life even better.

Accept the Reality of Your Situation

Before you can set course in a new direction you have to know where you're starting from. This first step will help you accept the reality that your marriage is over and everything that that reality means. You'll also have the chance to check out any defence mechanisms you may have that are preventing you from moving forward, and to work out exactly what went wrong in your relationship. Finally, you'll consider your practical, social and emotional responsibilities in the past, the present and, most importantly, the future.

CHAPTER 1

Accepting That It's Over

The first emotion experienced by pretty much everyone when their relationship ends is nothingness. Overwhelming nothingness. Whether you were the one who made the decision or the decision was forced on you, when those words 'we're over' were finally said, you probably felt very little at all. Feelings of numbness, emptiness and immobilisation are all normal reactions to a devastating and catastrophic event. Whether it's a global tragedy like a tsunami or earthquake, or the personal tragedy of a bereavement, the common human response is shock. We feel bewildered, disorientated and frozen – like the proverbial rabbit in the headlights.

Those who made the decision to end their relationship themselves can feel particularly confused by their reaction. The decision to separate may have been very difficult; nonetheless, they knew that their relationship was breaking down so surely the ending should have been predictable. However, the feeling of shock can still be intense.

Of course, there are some for whom the end of a relationship is a relief, but even in these cases, there can be difficult and confusing feelings to cope with. We invest so much of ourselves into our relationships, and it's often not until a relationship ends and we're confronted with the task of unravelling all the knots that bind us together that we realise how vast the challenge is.

Those knots might include practical things like financial responsibilities and a home, and emotional things such as a shared love for your children and other family members. You may have enjoyed an active social life, a shared passion for a hobby and joint goals for the future. Even if you hadn't been particularly close in recent years, your worlds were intertwined. Separating those worlds is a painful experience. Consequently, once the numbness of shock has begun to pass, many of us slip into the cosy oblivion of denial rather than face the emotional work that has to be done.

Denial is a common response after a separation, and one that gradually fades as the reality of the situation becomes clear. Rather than beginning to face the finality of divorce with all its fears and anxieties, however, many of us find a defence mechanism to hide behind. When our world has crashed it's natural to want to protect ourselves from emotional and psychological devastation, so we attempt to cut off that painful bit inside us like a bruise on an apple and throw it away so it can't hurt us. But in doing so, we lose a part of ourselves and run the risk of contamination creeping into the other areas of our life and creating long-term damage and decay.

The only healthy solution is to face the pain of ending and overcome it. In order to do that, we must switch off the individual defence mechanisms we each unconsciously employ that stop us accepting that our relationship is over.

RECOGNISING DEFENCE MECHANISMS

Defence mechanisms are normal and natural. As young children we learnt how to protect ourselves from overwhelming emotions so we didn't get hurt. We may have simply closed our eyes or put our fingers in our ears until the scary monster went away. When faced with a difficult or painful situation as an adult, our instincts tell us to do the same. Fortunately, however, most of us have discovered more sophisticated and far more subtle ways of protecting ourselves.

In healthy functioning adults, defence mechanisms are a short-term strategy to help us cope with an otherwise overwhelming situation. Once the frozen immobilisation of shock has worn off, our favoured defence mechanisms kick in while we get our psychological and emotional soldiers in a row ready to confront the problem. The purpose of the defence mechanism is to prevent psychological annihilation, particularly in the face of a sudden trauma. But once our psyche has had time to absorb the reality of the situation, we should gradually lower the defence and deal with the problem.

When confronted with a relationship breakdown, all of us will employ our favoured defence. Which technique we choose and develop will probably have been learnt from watching our parents manage life's crises. Depending on how successful we perceive the technique to be, we will have developed it further and personalised it for maximum personal benefit.

The following are common defences used during a relationship breakdown. You may fall into the trap of using just one of them, or you may use a different defence mechanism to manage different problems. Take a look at the list and see which applies most closely to you. If none of them seem to ring a bell, then you may be at the place in your recovery that no longer needs defences. Or you may be so deeply entrenched in your defence that you can't see it. If you're not sure, try chatting through this section with a trusted friend and see if they can open your eyes to anything.

DENIAL

Denial is a very common response to shock, but if it continues once the shock has worn off, then it may be being used as a defence mechanism. Denial is characterised by statements such as:

'He'll come back'
'It's just a phase'
'It's a trial separation – it won't last'

Denial doesn't want to accept the reality of what's going on in spite of the evidence to the contrary. Someone trapped in denial will constantly reassure themselves and others that the separation is only temporary. They will make no practical changes to their lifestyle because they don't believe there is any point. Many people in denial will tell very few people about the separation, and the few they do confide in will be told that although it's really painful, they're just going to ride the storm till things get back to normal.

Denial is the simplest and most straightforward of the defence mechanisms, but it potentially carries the highest price tag. As the weeks turn into months and the months turn into years, most deniers are forced to face the fact that the relationship is permanently over. When that reality hits, it's like a train crash. The full force of the pain is felt for the first time. Others around may wonder why it's taken so long for them to come to terms with the divorce but, in reality, the work had never even started.

MINIMISATION

Minimisation is a bit like denial but not quite so extreme as it's the pain of the situation that is denied rather than the fact that it's happened. A minimiser may say things like:

'It's not that bad, I'll be fine'
'I knew it wasn't working anyway so it's for the best'
'Divorce is so common nowadays, I'll cope fine'
'I didn't really love him anyway so I'm relieved he's gone'
'We can still be friends'

On the surface this may sound like optimism, but unlike an optimist, the sentiments are not heartfelt. Underneath these platitudes is an absolute terror of not coping. The unconscious plan is: 'if I keep telling myself I'm okay and it's not that bad, perhaps I'll eventually believe it'. A minimiser may seem to the world to be holding up very well, but when they're alone and/or under stress, the veneer may quickly crumble. Continuing to be friends could of course be a realistic goal, but if it's hung on to as a way of avoiding the pain of separation, it's a defence.

Like denial, minimisation is a common reaction soon after the news has been broken, but if you don't move on to look at the very real pain and struggle of separation, then you could be storing up problems for the future. Perhaps one of the saddest side-effects of minimisation is that it cuts us off from the support and comfort of others; and when the pain hits, which inevitably it will, many minimisers find themselves either alone or having to convince friends that they're not okay after all.

INTELLECTUALISATION

Intellectualisation is my favourite defence mechanism and one that therapists easily and naturally slip into. If you tend to cope with difficulties by intellectualising them, then you'll be a big fan of psychology and self-help books. Your friends will know you're an intellectualiser because you'll say things like:

> 'I've been thinking about why my partner left and I reckon it's because...'
> 'I've been thinking about how I've reacted to the separation and I think it's really interesting how I've...'

Rather than feel feelings, you analyse them. You ruminate and cogitate in a desperate attempt to develop understanding and find meaning. You may cry or shout sometimes, but mostly your head is far too busy trying to work things out.

Intellectualisation is a welcomed defence in a Western culture where strong displays of emotion are discouraged. We value the power of the mind and we advocate changing our thinking as a way of modulating our emotions. As with all defences, it's perfectly appropriate in the short term and in some circumstances to manage our feelings in this way. In the long term, however, if we're to ensure there's no unseen emotional leakage that will cause problems in the future, we need to address our emotional needs head-on.

ANGER

Anger is a natural reaction to any kind of loss, including the loss of a relationship (for more on anger, see Chapter 5). Occasionally, however, anger is employed early on in the grief process as a defence mechanism. Like the other defences, anger can protect us from looking at our deeper fears and insecurities. An angry defender will lose themselves into their rage to the exclusion of any other emotion. That rage may be directed at their ex, at themselves or at the person or event they perceive caused the end of the relationship. They may think things like:

> *'I hate her'*
> *'I'll never let him forget what he's done to me'*
> *'I'll never forgive myself for not...'*
> *'If it wasn't for the lover/job/bank we'd be fine'*

Anger is an incredibly destructive defence mechanism, not just to the individual, but also to those around them. It can feel energising and empowering, but all the focus tends to be externalised and in the past tense rather than focusing on the future and moving forward. It's often hard for friends to support the person trapped in anger as the tough, prickly exterior doesn't seem to invite any comfort or consolation. Consequently, many angry defenders are left feeling isolated and rejected by friends and family.

DISPLACEMENT

Displacement means packing up your feelings about something and projecting them onto something else. If it feels too dangerous or unsafe to experience and show our feelings in one place, we unconsciously find a safer outlet. For example, if you're angry with your boss for not giving you a promotion, you may smile politely at them then, when you get home, fly into a rage with your partner because they forgot the milk. Or you may not cry when you receive news of a debilitating illness, but find yourself sobbing through an episode of *Emmerdale*.

After a divorce or separation, the tidal wave of loss and pain may be displaced onto someone or something that's in its wake, rather than accepting the pain is yours. For example, all your emotional and psychological focus may go on your children, your job or even your ex. You may say things like:

> *'I'm okay, I'm just really worried about the kids'*
> *'I haven't got time to think about the divorce, I've got*
> *a major project at work and the company needs me'*
> *'I wish I could do something to make my ex feel*
> *better about what's happened'*

Displacement can be one of the more complicated defences to recognise as these concerns are often very valid and, in the case of children, things that should be worried about. But these things should not become concerns to the exclusion of an awareness of your own feelings and needs. The other problem with displacement is that you may be making something into much more of an issue for the person you're displacing onto. Your absolute conviction that your children or your ex can't cope may include an element of truth, but on top of that you're adding all of your own unacknowledged anxieties and pain for yourself. Consequently, they may end up feeling worse than they actually did, and receive all the sympathy and support of those around, leaving little to come your way.

REACTION FORMATION

This defence mechanism has the most unhelpful name but basically it's when a person decides to formulate their own positive reaction to a situation that most would find devastating. It goes beyond denial and minimisation into an almost euphoric opposite emotion. After a divorce or separation, reaction formation might sound something like this:

'I'm so pleased to finally have the house to myself'
'At last I'm rid of her – I've hated her for years'
'I'm so relieved it's over – it's the best thing that could have possibly happened'

Some of these statements may be true in part. A feeling of relief is common to many who've experienced relationship problems for a long time, but someone who's caught up in reaction formation will be unable to acknowledge anything but their joy at the separation. And whilst they're absorbed by their positive emotion, the equally real negative emotions remain unaddressed.

Reaction formation is a particularly difficult defence for those around to cope with, especially children who may be struggling to come to terms with losing a parent. Others may be astounded at the reaction and swing between believing and not believing. Unfortunately, this often has the effect of dividing family and friends, with some going along with the euphoric relief while others feel only the pain.

OVERCOMING DEFENCE MECHANISMS

In order to divorce healthily, you need to be sure that you're moving on from your defensive state and getting ready to face the future. Dropping a defence is a painful decision to make and one that may feel like emotional suicide, especially at first. In the long term, however, it really is the only way to start getting on with the rest of your life.

Whatever your defence, you need to take a long, hard look at the reality of your situation. It's perfectly understandable that you'll have fears and insecurities. There may be some days when you're able to look at them, and others when you hastily retreat back into your defence. Again, that's perfectly natural and it's important that you move forward in your own time.

A useful way of checking if you're ready to lower your defence is to do a cost/benefit analysis. All of our defences come at a cost: a cost to ourselves and a cost to others. By weighing up the costs and benefits of staying the same against the costs and benefits of dropping our defence, we can begin to make a positive decision to move on. On a sheet of paper, write your own personalised cost/benefit analysis. Try to make it as detailed as possible, thinking about all the ways that staying the same and changing affects you. Below is an example of how one client completed the exercise.

What are the costs/benefits of continuing with my minimisation defence mechanism?

	COSTS	BENEFITS
To myself	I won't ever face my fear of being a single parent and not finding anyone else who'll love me.	I can continue to feel in control of the situation and don't have to feel embarrassed and afraid of not coping.
To others	Friends don't know how much I'm hurting so they can't support me, which leaves me feeling even more alone. The kids are walking on eggshells around me.	I'm protecting my friends from knowing how difficult this all is for me.

What are the costs/benefits of overcoming my defence and facing the reality of my situation?

	COSTS	BENEFITS
To myself	It will hurt and I may need a few days off work.	I won't be so exhausted all the time and I'll be able to start addressing my fears rather than hiding from them.
To others	Some people may worry about me much more than they are at the moment.	People will be able to ask me how I am and I can honestly reply. The kids may feel more able to talk to me.

Whatever stage you're at in your separation, it's easy for your defence mechanisms to kick in without you noticing. There are so many hurdles along the path to a healthy divorce, and each of these can act as a trigger to set off a defence. But once you've acknowledged what your defence is, it's easier to overcome it and stop those psychological walls from being raised. Remember, defence mechanisms are a normal reaction to a difficult or painful situation, but the sooner you can lower them and address the issues they mask, the sooner you'll be back on the road to a healthy divorce.

CHAPTER 2

Understanding What Went Wrong

Why, why, why, why, why? Why did he leave me? Why didn't we talk about things sooner? Why didn't I see this coming? Why did I ever marry her? Why did he do this to me? Why was I so stupid? Why are we doing this?

For someone going through a divorce, questions like these are tormenting and endless. It's part of our nature to want to understand things, to find meaning for our experiences, especially our difficult experiences. For some, the pain of not knowing is so great that they grab hold of the nearest and most obvious answer like a drowning man grabbing a passing log. Unfortunately, this is often only part of the story, and clinging to it can take them further adrift from the truth.

Understanding why your relationship broke down is essential for a healthy divorce for two reasons. First, it enables you to silence the endless questions that keep you focusing on the past rather than thinking about the future. And second, it empowers you to approach future relationships with greater confidence.

At first glance, it may seem fairly obvious what went wrong in your relationship, especially if either you or your partner left for someone else or if you constantly argued about the same old issues. But these surface explanations rarely satisfy. Most of us need to know why our relationship was broken by a third party or irresolvable difference when other marriages survive these challenges. There's often a nagging doubt that there's a deeper, more fundamental explanation. And in most cases, there is.

All relationships hit problems. All couples argue. Many couples are tempted by an affair and a few succumb to the temptation. But most marriages survive. The difference between those that make it and those that break is what Relate relationship counsellors call the 'fit'. All couples 'fit' together for a number of reasons. Some of those reasons will be conscious ones, such as sharing similar hobbies, values and hopes for the future. Others will be less conscious, such as a shared difficulty in managing anger and conflict, or an unspoken agreement to always look on the bright side of life. This fit may stay the same throughout a couple's relationship while others may change, with varying degrees of discomfort and upheaval. But the common denominator in almost all relationship breakdowns is that either one or both of you broke the fit and you've been unable to negotiate a new one.

RECOGNISING YOUR ORIGINAL FIT

Our relationship fit starts when we first meet. While our heart and eyelashes are fluttering, our head is running down our internal wish list and checking out if Mr or Miss Could-be-Right ticks enough boxes. If they do, and assuming we tick enough of theirs, the relationship fit will begin to evolve. As the weeks and months pass and we get to know more and more about our partner, the fit will expand to include all the unspoken messages that we pick up. Some of these messages will match our own while others will complement our shortcomings.

For example, one client, James, explained how he had fallen in love with his wife Jeanette because of her quiet strength and resilience, and her amazing ability to put the needs of others before her own. He said that she had loved him for his independence, ambition and the fact that he could always make her laugh. They also shared a lot of the same friends and both dreamed of being successful and having a large family. The original fit had been their mutual interests and goals, and a deeper unspoken agreement that James would be the independent, confident provider and Jeanette would be the quiet, resourceful caregiver. They'd also made an unspoken deal that rather than discussing and getting upset by anything in life, James would see the funny side of it and Jeanette would smile and soldier on. James admitted that as an only child brought up in a family that never had a cross word, he was terrified of conflict; and he quickly recognised that Jeanette, the eldest of five in a family that fought constantly, was exactly the same. He also realised that he'd always secretly envied Jeanette's self-sacrificing personality as it was so different to his self-centred approach to the world.

Like most couples, James and Jeanette's original fit worked well for them for many years. It wasn't until their marriage broke down that James began to consider the impact of their original, largely unspoken contract.

Sometimes the unconscious fit is much more obvious to outsiders than it is to ourselves, such as when the social butterfly falls for the strong silent type. The unconscious fit is 'I'll be sociable for you while you're self-sufficient for me'. Other classic examples of how opposites attract and find and act out their missing part through the other include the creative person falling for the rules-and-regulations type, or the fiery maternal protector falling for little boy lost. In these cases it is often the thing that attracted us most when we first met that annoys us most when we finally separate.

We also know that birds of a feather flock together. Others might have noticed long ago that both of you struggled with low self-esteem or anxiety, or had a shared loathing of displays of strong emotion. Together you may have unconsciously colluded to keep certain things out of your relationship so that neither of you had to confront your fears.

You may find it helpful to write down the things that made you and your partner fall in love, both the conscious things that attracted you to each other, and the unspoken agreements that you made. Think about the things you had in common with your partner that were important to you when you met, and the aspects of each other's personality that you found particularly attractive. Did your partner have qualities that you wished you'd had yourself? Think also about the way you managed your relationship in the early days, particularly in terms of how you handled differences and conflict.

Here's an example of what one client, Lorraine, wrote:

I loved my partner because… *He was caring, intelligent, laid-back, funny and had loads of friends. He was sensitive to my needs and looked after me. I felt special when I was with him.*

My partner loved me because… *I was independent, attractive and organised. He said he liked the fact that I didn't make a fuss about trivial things but would stand up for the things I believed in.*

Our original fit was… *a shared dream of a house by the sea and running our own business. He never had any strong opinions so tended to let me get on with my own thing and make decisions for both of us. We were both very laid-back about differences because we respected each other's autonomy. We rarely rowed because he used to get really upset if I got angry and that used to stop me in my tracks.*

Every couple will have their own original fit and, like James and Jeanette, it will have worked, at least for a while. Some couples go many years with few obstacles to challenge their fit, while others hit a catalogue of problems early on. Either way, most couples have to face the fact that both life and people change. And when they do, they must reappraise and renegotiate the very foundation of their relationship.

WHEN THE FIT BEGINS TO CHANGE

Few of us are exactly the same as we were when we first met our partners. Aside from a few wrinkles and a few extra pounds, most of us will be more self-aware and wiser about the workings of the world. Life's experiences, both good and bad, will have left their mark. Your job may have changed how you feel about yourself, and if you've had children, you'll have discovered many aspects of your personality that you never knew existed. As we grow as individuals, our relationship has to change to accommodate our new thoughts, feelings and behaviours. How you manage – or don't manage – those changes is the key to understanding what went wrong.

'Fifteen years into our marriage, life was peachy,' said James in one of his counselling sessions. He was managing director of his own very successful manufacturing business, and Jeanette was working part-time as a language tutor and looking after their four boys. The only things they argued about were her low sex drive and him not giving enough time and attention to the boys when he was home. The sex issue got to him a lot as he interpreted this as selfishness on Jeanette's part. On the numerous occasions when he'd tried to get to the bottom of what was wrong, she refused to talk about it, which annoyed him even more.

Changes in relationship fit often creep up slowly and gradually and leak out in ongoing arguments over what may seem like an unrelated matter. Underneath most arguments about money, housework, children, sex and life-work balance are deeper needs that are not being met, needs that you thought you'd agreed upon in your unspoken contract. For some couples, a sudden crisis might fast-forward the process. For example, if a couple's fit had been 'I'll be the strong one and look after you', an illness or bereavement could devastate that agreement. Or an unfair dismissal or other miscarriage of justice might catapult the 'I'm laid-back' person into a seemingly uncharacteristic course of action.

You may want to write down when things began to change for you in your relationship. Before doing so, think about the things that happened in each of your lives and how that changed your thoughts, feelings and attitudes to yourself, each other and life in general. This is what Lorraine wrote about how things began to change in her relationship:

> Our fit began to change when... *I had my first baby and needed him to be around more and spend more time with me. My career was not working out as I'd hoped so I was less confident than I used to be. He got a promotion at work and started spending more time with workmates and became more argumentative. We started rowing more often but never resolved anything because I'd get angry and he'd storm out.*

For some people, change is easy – for others it's terrifying. When things begin to change in your relationship, it can be totally unnerving and, unfortunately, many couples find it difficult to negotiate those changes healthily. The inability to change tends to lead to one of two conclusions: either you continue to have endless arguments which never reach a resolution or you grow further and further apart.

WHEN THE FIT BREAKS

This is the bottom line of your relationship breakdown. The trigger to separate may have been an affair, a particularly bad row, a significant disappointment or an external event that seems unrelated, but what went wrong was that you no longer 'fitted' together. One or both of you changed in some way that broke the original contract. That change may not necessarily have been in a bad way – indeed many changes are positive. For example, someone who learns to be more assertive or gets in touch with their emotions will need their partner to accommodate the difference, but this will require a change in the partner too. It's not possible for one part of a relationship to change without it impacting the other.

James realised that Jeanette had changed. She had become increasingly vocal about her needs and demanded that he became less work orientated and selfish. He knew he'd changed too. He wanted to talk about more personal stuff, not just their sexual problems but also difficulties at work. Jeanette accused him of becoming 'heavy' and laughed at him if he tried to talk about these things. Unfortunately, neither of them had learnt how to manage conflict so, if either of them got angry, they just retreated into silence. Finally, after 19 years of marriage, Jeanette had an affair. James was stunned. He'd suspected something was going on as she'd become more and more angry about him not being there for the boys and sex was non-existent, but he never thought she'd do this.

Looking back at your relationship in this way may help you to see that the cracks began to appear a long time ago. Like James, you may have tried to address some of them, but your partner wouldn't or couldn't manage the change. Some partners change so much or in a particular way that it is impossible for the other partner to adapt. For example, if one partner decides they no longer want children, or they want a non-monogamous relationship, or they become violent. In situations like these the price of changing to adapt to a partner's needs may come at far too high a cost, a cost that would mean losing a sense of themselves. Sometimes a partner cannot adapt to any kind of change in their partner, and while they stay exactly the same as they were when they first married, their partner changes almost unrecognisably. When either of these situations happen, a split is almost inevitable.

The final exercise for you to complete in this section is to think about how you have changed from the person you were when you first got together, and how your partner has changed. Finally, consider how these changes caused your relationship to fail. In your notebook answer 'I changed by…', 'My partner changed by…' and 'Our relationship failed because…' This is what Lorraine wrote:

> I changed by: *becoming more dependent on him and needing him to affirm me more. I wasn't the strong independent person he fell in love with.*
>
> My partner changed by: *becoming more absorbed in his career and more independent. He wanted to spend more time with his friends and seemed to put everything before me. He was no longer the sensitive, caring man I fell in love with.*
>
> Our relationship failed because: *we never learnt how to have a proper argument so we couldn't sort out our differences. And because I need someone who'll be sensitive when I'm vulnerable, and he needs someone who's independent and can cope alone and not put too many demands on him.*

As you may have noticed in the case of James and Jeanette, and that of Lorraine, no one was really to blame. In most relationship breakdowns, the fault does not lie solely with either individual. Each must accept some responsibility for the changes they made or didn't make, and the way they adapted or didn't adapt to accommodate each other. Relationships are like dancing. When you first meet you learn each other's steps and combine them so you can dance together in perfect synchrony. When one of you learns new steps, you have to re-choreograph the dance so you don't get out of sync. If you don't, you'll end up stepping on each other's toes or drifting apart. Eventually, if you can't get back in step, one of you may decide you'd prefer either to dance solo or find a new dance partner. Neither of you has failed; the relationship has.

CHAPTER 3

Taking Your Share of the Responsibility

In a long-term relationship, most responsibilities are shared. We may divide up the tasks, but the overall responsibilities are mutual. Most couples have a shared responsibility for providing a home, generating an income, looking after children and other family members and looking after each other. When a couple split, those responsibilities have to be split as well.

This is often much easier said than done, especially when emotions are involved. However, when we can truly accept our responsibility for the past, the present and the future, we can begin to untangle some of the emotional bonds that still tie us to our ex. We can also gain a much greater sense of control and self-determination. When something is our responsibility – not someone else's – it's up to us what we do with it, and it's within our power to change it for the better.

We can break down our responsibilities into three key areas – practical, social and emotional. In each of these areas, we can choose to see the responsibility as a burden that limits and ties us down or as a liberation, something that gives us new options and frees us to make our own choices.

PRACTICAL RESPONSIBILITIES

YOUR HOME

Home is where the heart is, or so the saying goes. After a divorce, it may feel like your home is no longer your own, or indeed you may find yourself having to look for a new one. For many couples, the home was a joint refuge, a place for relaxation and recuperation. Most of us need somewhere we can retreat from the world and feel safe. Whatever your circumstances now, you have a responsibility to yourself to make yourself a new home where you can truly feel *at* home.

If you have children, you also have a responsibility to create a home for them. Whether they will live with you or not, you have a duty to ensure they have somewhere safe and comfortable to live, and somewhere safe and comfortable to stay when they're with the non-resident parent.

EMPLOYMENT AND FINANCES

If you have children to support, then the decisions you make about employment and finances will obviously affect them too. Assuming you're able as parents to provide the agreed basics – for example a home, living essentials, education – then how you earn and spend any surplus money is up to you. For many people, both with and without children, divorce is an opportunity to change career or change their work-life balance. Some may choose to work further afield, change their hours or retrain to do something completely new. The advantage of this becoming solely your responsibility is that it is now totally your choice.

PHYSICAL HEALTH

You may have always taken personal responsibility for your health. Like many, however, you may have needed your partner's encouragement to get regular exercise, or their culinary expertise to eat healthily. Some people slip into bad lifestyle habits when they're in a relationship and make little effort to keep themselves in good physical condition. For them, a divorce can be a trigger to begin a new health regime. Others may have kept themselves fit and healthy for a partner and see little point in continuing once they're single, but this kind of thinking can lead to increased feelings of stress and low self-esteem.

We now know that our bodies react better to stress when they're in optimum condition. Divorce is a very stressful time by anyone's standards, so it's particularly important to look after yourself now. As well as managing stress better, you're also more likely to feel good about yourself if you're happy with how you look. Now you're alone, it's up to you to optimise your health and appearance. What you eat, how much you sleep, how much exercise you do, the clothes you wear and how you do your hair – all these things are your choice and your responsibility.

There are many other practical responsibilities, such as maintaining a car, looking after pets, running a business or holiday home, and much more. Take time to list all the practical responsibilities you need to be aware of as you move on in your life.

SOCIAL RESPONSIBILITIES

FAMILY

Families come in many shapes and sizes. Some are close geographically and emotionally, while others are more distant. When you married you may have been warmly welcomed into your partner's family, and if you have children, then you will always have a shared connection to grandparents. It's not possible, or indeed advantageous, to split the family back into its separate compartments after a divorce, especially if you have children. If your divorce has been very acrimonious then rifts may have already occurred, but if they haven't you must now decide how and with whom you keep in touch. While making these decisions it's essential that you think about the long-term as well as the short-term consequences, and ensure that you're not making any decisions based on transient negative emotions.

FRIENDS

It's very common in couple relationships for one partner to look after the friendships and the social calendar. Divorce often catapults people in two opposite directions. Some cut themselves off from people altogether, while others will do anything to avoid being alone. Both of these extremes are unhealthy. In order to maintain good mental health, you need to find the right balance of alone time and time with friends and family (see page 186 for further advice). Spend some time thinking about the friendships that are important to you and how you can maintain them.

HOBBIES, PASTIMES AND PERSONAL DEVELOPMENT

If you weren't the busy, sociable one in your relationship then you might never have considered having hobbies of your own. You might have been happy enough accompanying your partner in their interests, or found yourself too exhausted by all their activity to do anything for yourself. Now you're alone, you need to consider what kind of things you want to do. Many people find that divorce leaves time on their hands, and a great antidote to boredom and loneliness is to take responsibility for finding a new interest or activity. That could be something as simple as reading more or going for walks, or it could be taking up a new physical or creative challenge. It really doesn't matter what it is as long as it's something that interests you.

Other social responsibilities might include spending time with work colleagues, continuing with a sport or other recreational activity, and taking holidays and family days out. Take time to brainstorm and note down all the social and recreational areas that you'd like to continue, develop or expand.

EMOTIONAL RESPONSIBILITIES

I have deliberately left this section till last as it is potentially the most delicate and complicated area to cover. Accepting responsibility for our emotions may seem obvious to some, but if a divorce has been particularly painful or acrimonious, it's easy to continue to blame a partner and hold them responsible for how we feel. Furthermore, it's easy to fall into the trap of blaming our behaviour on an ex, saying that we have no choice in how we behave because of the way an ex has made us feel. Not only does this kind of thinking leave you emotionally tied to your ex but it also robs you of the power to change your circumstances. You cannot begin to move on healthily in your divorce until you accept that you are responsible for your own emotions and consequently have the ultimate control over them (see Step Two for more about managing difficult emotions).

YOUR DAILY FEELINGS

If you think about it logically, no one can make you feel something. I cannot make you feel angry, sad, lonely or anxious. If I were to say or do something to you, your response might be to feel one of these things, but that would be your choice, not mine. For example, if I said 'You're an idiot', you might feel angry, hurt, bemused, confused or just indifferent. When feelings seem out of control, it's sometimes difficult to believe that it's not someone else controlling them, but if people really could make us feel something, why wouldn't our friends and family make us feel happy? Undoubtedly, they try on a regular basis but they can't. They can't because it's simply not possible to make someone feel something unless they want to. Ultimately, we are always responsible for our emotions.

POSITIVE SELF-WORTH

Feelings of low self-worth are common during a divorce – for those who feel rejected, those who are struggling with guilt and those who are finding it difficult to cope. You need to accept that *your* self-esteem is *your* responsibility (see Chapter 7 for advice on boosting your self-esteem). However close you may have been to your ex, and however much you valued their opinion and affirmation of you, now you're alone it's your job to fill that gap and boost your own ego.

OPTIMISM

Many couples consist of an optimist and a pessimist. Regardless of which one you may have been in the past, you may be struggling to be optimistic now. If you were always the optimist battling with a pessimistic partner, you may find that now there's no one there to take the negative view for you, you're being forced to take it alone. And if you were the pessimist, you may see divorce as proof that you were right all along. Either way, it's up to you to decide how full the glass is and to hold the hope for your future.

SUPPORTING OTHERS

This may seem like an odd thing to put under emotional responsibility, but for many of us, supporting other people – particularly children or aging parents – is part of our life. When times are tough and you're feeling worn out, it's understandable to struggle to support others, and it may be wise to ask for additional support for yourself. What's more important, however, is to acknowledge that your responsibility to others is not diminished by your divorce, and your partner cannot be blamed for carelessness or thoughtlessness. Regardless of what may have happened to your relationship, you still have a responsibility to be a good parent or daughter or whatever your role may be. Make a list now of your emotional responsibilities.

THE FAILURE OF YOUR MARRIAGE

This may be the toughest emotional responsibility for you to face – and, of course, it's highly unlikely that you will be taking *all* of the responsibility yourself. As we saw in the previous chapter, most relationships break down because the individuals fail to keep in step with each other. The changes often

35

occur over a long period of time until something happens that triggers the final decision to separate. Having worked through the previous chapter, you may have come to the conclusion that your only responsibility was that you didn't see it coming sooner. You may have been so absorbed in other commitments and interests that you didn't notice that your relationship was changing. Or perhaps you did notice, but you didn't do anything about it, hoping that it would get better on its own. Or you may have tried to talk to your partner on endless occasions, but failed. If for some reason you were unable to feel heard in your relationship, you may decide that you need to take some responsibility for that breakdown in communication. If you were the victim of domestic violence, or another form of abuse, then it's important that you know that you were not to blame for your situation. Your only responsibility may have been making the decision to be with that person in the first place.

I would suggest that you now write down the ways that you were responsible for the breakdown of your marriage. The object of doing this is not to place blame at your door, but to enable you to feel more confident about future relationships. Once you can accept your share of the reasons why the marriage failed, then you can make positive choices to make different decisions next time. Of course, it's too late to change the past, but it's never too late to have a better future.

Congratulations on completing Step One. I hope that you now have a much better understanding of what went wrong in your relationship and any defences that you need to work through to help you to move on. Your list of responsibilities can serve as a reminder for you of the things you need to consider as you continue to work through this book.

Manage Your Emotions

This step will help you to manage the bewildering roller coaster of emotions that we confront when a relationship breaks down. Starting with grief and fear, we will look at how you can feel more in control of your feelings of loss. The section on anger will help you to analyse whether your anger is helping or hindering you, and looks at how you can make anger a positive force in your life. The final section focuses on how you can free yourself from doubts, regret and guilt, enabling you to look at your future with confidence.

CHAPTER 4

Coping with Grief and Fear

After losing his wife, C. S. Lewis said, 'No one ever told me that grief felt so like fear. I am not afraid, but the sensation is like being afraid. The same fluttering in the stomach, the same restlessness.'

This has been the experience of many people. Both grief and fear can be overwhelming and paralysing, and both are common responses to losing someone you loved. A relationship breakdown is one of life's most painful experiences and the feelings of loss can be profound. If the break-up was against your wishes and unexpected, then your experience may be particularly acute. But even those who initiated the separation can struggle with powerful feelings of grief. This is because we invest so much of ourselves in our intimate relationships – emotionally, physically and spiritually. Even if a relationship has been unfulfilling or difficult for some time, there is still loss. We may not grieve for the person, but we have to give up all our hopes and dreams of being able to make the relationship work. We are forced to let go – not just of the past, but of the future as well.

If your relationship has been a long one, then you may also feel that you're losing part of your identity – your role as a wife or husband, as a lover and friend and perhaps also your role as a resident parent. You may also be losing your home, your standard of living, certain friendships, in-laws and some of your possessions. For many, their basic sense of security is lost, and with it their self-confidence and self-worth. When a relationship breaks up, many people feel that they are breaking down as both their internal and external worlds begin to separate.

The light amid what may seem like an all-consuming darkness, however, is the knowledge that people can, and do, survive divorce. It may feel like hell, but in fact it's only purgatory because it does come to an end.

WHY SOME PEOPLE COPE BETTER THAN OTHERS

The circumstances of the separation are of huge significance to how you'll manage the break-up and how long it will take you to recover. Generally speaking, shorter relationships are easier to recover from as roles and identities as a couple are not so firmly established. However, this is not always the case as a shorter relationship may still be viewed in an idealised way, and the ending may come as an even greater shock. Recovery is also likely to be quicker where there has been an awareness and acknowledgement of difficulties, though some people may be left hurt and frustrated if they were not given the chance to try to resolve them.

Another significant factor is an individual's experience of loss in the past. Sometimes the end of a loving relationship can bring back powerful memories of earlier separation and loss. This could be the ending of a previous couple relationship or an earlier loss. Childhood losses – whether of a parent through bereavement or separation, or an emotional loss due to abuse or addiction – are often pushed deep into our unconscious mind. A later loss can trigger those unconscious memories and make the current crisis much harder to manage. In short, previous loss can complicate the grief process and make the pain more acute. Conversely, many people who have experienced and recovered from multiple losses recover faster as they have already developed the resources and techniques they need to move forward.

When Grief Turns to Depression

Grief is a normal and healthy response to loss. In most cases, with time and the support of friends and family, it will reach a natural conclusion. However, sometimes grief can trigger depression. If your feelings of emptiness and sadness continue to be overwhelming for more than six months, and you feel no pleasure at any time – and if these feelings are accompanied by any of the following – then you should consult your GP to talk about additional medical support:

➤ Changes in appetite or weight
➤ Inability to sleep or oversleeping
➤ Constant tiredness and lack of energy
➤ Problems concentrating or remembering things
➤ Physical restlessness and twitchiness or feeling physically slow or sluggish
➤ Suicidal thoughts or feelings

EASING THE PAIN

Time really is the greatest healer, but there are some things you can do to speed up the clock. Below is a list of things that Relate counsellors often suggest to help the grief process:

➤ Take care of yourself physically. Eat regular, healthy meals and take regular exercise. Indulging in comfort food and slumping on the sofa all day adds to negative feelings.

➤ Talk. It doesn't matter who you talk to – a trusted friend, family member or next-door neighbour – talking prevents isolation and puts us in touch with the many other people who've been in the same situation.

➤ Keep fond memories. When something happens that makes you feel sad, such as hearing a song or seeing a photograph, try to focus on the happiness you once felt rather than on the sadness you now feel.

➤ Let yourself cry. There will be some days when you just want to give up and cry, and that's okay. You need to be real about how you feel and give yourself permission to express those emotions. And when you're angry, let out those feelings too. Keeping powerful feelings bottled up tends to make things much worse and can stop you from moving forward.

➤ Think ahead. On a bad day, it's easy to think that you'll feel like this for ever. Making yourself think ahead to what you'd like to be doing when you're over this can help to kick-start your optimism (see Step Seven for more on this).

➤ Relax. Relaxation will help your body to de-stress. You could read a book, watch a DVD, go for a walk or have a soak in the bathtub. If you're quite an active person, go for a run, work out in the gym, kick a ball around or do some gardening to relax.

➤ Treat yourself. Take any opportunity you can to give yourself a treat. That might be something as simple as a cup of tea, listening to a new CD or enjoying a foot soak, or you might really push the boat out and have a professional massage or weekend away.

Grief can feel overwhelming as all the losses get rolled into one and we can struggle to maintain perspective. Writing a list of the different things that you'll miss can help make the pain feel easier to cope with. Rather than experiencing the pain as one massive lump, you can break it down into smaller, more manageable pieces. The pain can also cloud our ability to remember that the relationship wasn't always good. In reality, there will almost certainly be a list of things that you *won't* miss. These may be things about your ex's character, your lifestyle together or specific difficulties and tensions in the relationship. Making a note of these can help you to keep your feelings of grief balanced.

Here is an example of what Alan wrote:

I will miss...

Someone to talk to when I get home
Someone to relax with in the evening
My home
Putting the kids to bed every night
Hearing about their day at school
Having dinner cooked
Her support and advice on problems
Her mum and dad
Someone to go on holiday with
The security of being intimately known

I won't miss...

Her moaning and nagging
Having to live up to her tidiness standards
The noise of the kids bickering
Her telling me I wasn't good enough
Some of her cooking
Not knowing if or when she'd leave me
Living in town
Driving so far to work every day
Watching endless soaps
The arguments
Pretending to the boys that everything was okay

Not every cloud has a silver lining, but many of them do if we look hard enough. Every relationship has problems, and consequently there will always be at least some advantages to being out of it. That's not to say that the grief of much of your loss isn't great, but holding the perspective of there also being some gains can help you to cope better.

At the beginning of this chapter we saw how grief and fear often feel the same. Some losses will trigger significant anxieties about the future, and while many of these anxieties may be real, others will be unfounded. However, just because a fear may be unfounded, or even irrational, doesn't make it any less terrifying. Consider, for example, many people's fear of the dark or of spiders. Knowing that there is no logical reason to be afraid often isn't enough to make the feeling subside. This is because fear is one of humankind's primary emotions, essential to our survival. In order to overcome our fears, we need to repeatedly convince ourselves that there is no threat and we will survive.

In spite of what the media may tell us, we actually need very little to survive. We will not die if we don't have the latest gadget, age-defying cream, nutritional snack, home, holiday or car. Indeed, there's no reason why we can't live perfectly happy and fulfilled lives without them. Similarly, the media has sold us the lie that true happiness is found in living happily ever after with the romantic partner of your dreams. However, as an increasing number of happy singletons will tell you, this simply isn't true. Whatever your fears may be telling you right now, you can be happy again, either because your losses will be replaced or restored, or because you'll learn to live contentedly without them.

Your fears and anxieties may be on behalf of others. For example, you might worry about how your ex will cope or about your children. Again, in reality, nobody really dies from a broken heart, and although divorce and separation do have an impact on children, that impact can be minimised. Many children bear witness to being stronger and more mature individuals as a result of the experience.

OVERCOMING FEAR AND ANXIETY

The first step towards overcoming fear and anxiety is to name it. Many of us struggle for years under a nagging weight of impending doom without ever confronting what the anxiety is really about. It's a bit like the small child who grips tightly onto her duvet every night, worrying that something might be under the bed. Once you've named what could be under the bed, you can ask yourself what the likelihood is of it really being there and then finally take a look and see for yourself.

Take the opportunity now to write your own list of fears. You may find that looking back over your list of losses will help you to name some of the nagging anxieties that you're unclear about. Try to be as honest and succinct as you can. List the big fears and the little worries, and even if you know it's irrational, put it down. Here's what Alan's list looked like:

I'm afraid of...
Being lonely
Not meeting someone else
Missing out on the boys' childhood
Not settling into a new home
Losing friends
Becoming a hermit
Living on ready meals for ever
Never having sex again
Having no money
Losing my job

In the vast majority of cases, fears are 'what ifs' and 'maybes'. Divorce confronts us with an unknown future, and it is part of our natural instinct to be cautious of the unknown. But once we confront the 'what ifs' and reality-check them, we can focus our attention on ensuring the dreaded fear doesn't happen.

So, now you can go to your list and give each item a score between 1 and 10 for how probable it is that this will happen. Use 10 to indicate that it's very probable and 1 that it's highly improbable. Once you've done this, go back through the list and score each item between 1 and 10 for how much power you have to prevent it from happening. Finally, complete the third column, scoring each item for the impact it has on your life, using 10 to indicate a high impact and 1 for minimal impact. Here's how Alan's final list looked:

	Probability of it happening (1–10)	My power to avoid (1–10)	Impact on my life (1–10)
Being lonely	3	7	10
Not meeting someone else	5	5	8
Missing out on the boys' childhood	3	10	8
Not settling into a new home	2	8	6
Losing friends	8	2	4
Becoming a hermit	3	10	8
Living on ready meals for ever	1	10	1
Never having sex again	4	7	4
Having no money	5	7	4
Losing my job	7	2	8

As you can see, in most cases the probability was actually very low and Alan's power to avoid the situation happening was very high. He was also surprised when he noted down the impact that the fear actually had on his life. He had lived with very little money in the past so financial hardship wasn't really a major issue for him. However, although the chance of being lonely was relatively low and his power to avoid it was high, he realised that it would have a massive impact on him. He was also able to see the areas where things were more out of his control. His company had already experienced a number of redundancies leading up to his divorce so losing his job was a real possibility. He also knew that one friend was particularly angry with him about the marriage break-up and might decide to withhold contact.

Doing this exercise can help you get a much better grip on which of your fears are rational and which are less so. With this increased knowledge, you can begin to face and overcome the less rational fears by challenging and changing the negative thinking patterns that sustain them.

Generally speaking, negative thinking precedes negative emotions. If we consistently tell ourselves that we cannot cope then we won't. If we lock ourselves in our homes and say we'll never meet someone else then the 'what if' fear will become a reality. Stopping this negative thinking takes effort and discipline, but it is possible. The bigger fears may take longer to overcome, and part of this process may require looking at the worst-case scenario and working out how you'll manage if it happens. But whether your fears and anxieties are big or small, rational or irrational, all of them are challenges that can be overcome, one way or another.

Steps Three, Four and Five focus specifically on these and other challenges that you'll face during and after your divorce, and provide you with practical ways of overcoming them.

CHAPTER 5

Overcoming Anger and Resentment

Anger is a natural and normal response to any kind of loss. Whether you lose your car keys or lose your spouse, some degree of frustration, irritation or rage is inevitable. But anger is not always a bad thing. Anger can be a very positive emotion, one that motivates us to protect, survive and fight for our rights and the rights of others. Or anger can be negative, keeping us trapped and hurting, damaging our health and alienating others.

The roots of anger – whether healthy or not – are pretty much the same. We tend to feel angry when:

➤ Our rights have been denied
➤ We've been cheated, abused, rejected, insulted or humiliated
➤ Our goals have been thwarted
➤ A personal rule has been broken
➤ Our self-esteem is threatened

Unfortunately, the average relationship breakdown could tick all of those five points. Many people feel severely battered and abused by divorce – if not by their ex, then by the legal system and the struggles and pressures of being single. That anger might be turned outwards towards an ex, a third party or event that triggered the separation, or the legal and social system that may seem to be thwarting their attempts for fairness. Sometimes the anger is turned inwards on the self, resulting in endless self-reproach, blame and, eventually, depression. Even though anger may be inevitable, however, how we respond to it is not. Each of us has a personal responsibility, as we saw in the last chapter, to decide how we will react to and express our emotions. If we choose to respond healthily, then anger may be used as a catalyst for change; but if the anger is unhealthy, then it will end up doing us much more harm than good.

HEALTHY VERSUS UNHEALTHY ANGER

Healthy anger may feel intense, but it's controlled. It may feel slightly uncomfortable, but is nothing that cannot be handled or switched off when required. Healthy anger leads to positive, respectful decisions that assert your rights. It is achieved by recognising that life is not always fair, and you may not always be treated well, but in spite of that, you choose to react in line with your own standards of behaviour. Healthy anger is energising and motivating and can be harnessed to create positive change (see page 52).

Unhealthy anger tends to feel overwhelming and dominate our thinking. It is more likely to be expressed aggressively or even violently, or it may leak out in passive-aggressive behaviour and a constant feeling of irritability with the world and everyone in it. Unhealthy anger is fed by negative thinking and by holding on to rigid beliefs that the world should be fair and people should behave in a certain way. It also assumes that there is clear right and wrong in the world, and usually that you're the one in the right. On top of this is an assumption that if someone or something gets in the way of your plans, it's deliberate and it's personal. Unhealthy anger is also more likely to plot revenge and be expectantly waiting for further offences.

IS YOUR ANGER HEALTHY OR UNHEALTHY?

Having read the descriptions of healthy and unhealthy anger, you may already know which sort of anger you most commonly experience. If not, you may find the following exercise useful to help you decide exactly what you're feeling.

Is My Anger Generally Healthy or Unhealthy?
Using the score sheet below, circle the answers that are most true about you.

I feel angry when...	Often	Occasionally	Never
People don't do what I expect them to	5	3	1
I am spoken to in a disrespectful or rude way	5	3	1
Something gets in the way of my plans	5	3	1
I am made to feel stupid or ignorant	5	3	1
I'm left feeling vulnerable and afraid	5	3	1
Other people don't make allowances for me	5	3	1
The world is unfair and unjust	5	3	1
Life is more complicated than it should be	5	3	1

If you scored over 28 then your anger is often unhealthy. If you scored under 20 then your anger is mostly healthy. If you scored somewhere in between then look at the areas where you scored highly and use the ABCDE technique (see page 57) to change those unhealthy anger situations to healthy ones.

ACCEPTING IMPERFECTION

The bottom line in overcoming unhealthy anger is to realise that life is not perfect and all humans are fallible. There are very few rules in life. It's not a rule that people should be nice to you and always treat you with respect. It is, of course, a courtesy but it's not a rule, and there will always be people who do not see common courtesy as important. Life is also often unfair. Shit happens! And unfortunately, sometimes you'll be in the firing line.

If you've suffered a lot of misfortunes in life then it's easy to be pessimistic and to begin to develop a persecution complex. In reality, though, very few people deliberately go out of their way to harm someone, but because of their failings and weaknesses, sometimes they will hurt others. And, of course, the same is also true of us.

During a divorce, it's particularly easy to assume that your ex has it in for you. Indeed, on some occasions you may be right. If your partner is angry and bitter with you, then they may be attempting to sabotage your happiness and undermine your rights. Even in these cases, however, you can choose to turn this into healthy anger which accepts that your ex is not perfect, and because of their pain they're temporarily not being fair. You can decide to turn this healthy anger into a motivating energy to help you ensure your rights and needs are fulfilled, or you can respond with unhealthy anger and face the consequences.

THE CONSEQUENCES OF UNHEALTHY ANGER

Anger has been described as a cancer. While others may see a few symptoms on the outside, most of the damage is internal. As the anger slowly eats away at its victim's life, not only does it steal a person's joy and happiness but it also keeps its victim trapped in the past. Any unresolved, negative emotion ties you to your ex, but anger is by far the strongest and most powerful bond.

If anger is continually fed by persistent negative thinking, it will grow, slowly and painfully, until it morphs into long-standing resentment. Resentment can be just as damaging as anger – often more so in fact. Anger may ebb and flow, whereas resentment tends to remain constant. Resentment also ties us to the past, but it often has another consequence – immobility. Because resentment tends to be constant it can easily feel like a permanent state. Therefore, it's easy to feel trapped and unable to move forward. As the frustration builds at being trapped, many people inadvertently escalate the situation by getting even angrier with themselves or their ex for making them so angry. This quickly becomes a vicious cycle of resentment – blame – immobilisation – resentment – blame – immobilisation.

Unhealthy anger may be loud and aggressive, damaging innocent bystanders and alienating friends and family. It's also been associated with health issues such as raised blood pressure and heart problems. Sometimes unhealthy anger is cold, quiet and simmering, turned inwards rather than out. This latter type of anger is often more acceptable in our society but it's equally powerful at keeping its victim feeling trapped and alone. Common health consequences include headaches, digestive problems and depression.

Making the decision to let go of your anger can free you to move forward. It can enable you to put your energies towards more positive activities such as creating a home, being a parent, building a career, establishing your independence or finding a new partner. You'll smile more and laugh more, and you'll probably attract more friends and potential dates, as you'll be fun to be around. Your health will improve and, if the aging experts are to be believed, you'll look younger as you produce more feel-good chemicals. How could anyone resist!

WHY PEOPLE HANG ON TO THEIR ANGER

The reason so many of us have a problem with letting go of our anger is that we believe we have a right to be angry. We believe our anger is justified. They, it, she, he, or even ourselves, deserve our anger. Not being angry may be seen as a weakness or a failure. We may be letting ourselves down and letting them off the hook. In reality, the only person we're really letting off the hook is ourselves, but until we challenge our negative thinking pattern, we're not going to see it that way. Here are some of the most common reasons people give for hanging on to their anger.

My Anger is Justified

This is the number one explanation given for continuing to hold on to anger, but in reality, it's a bit of a red herring. If your anger is indeed justified, and perhaps it is, ask yourself if it's a positive or negative force in your life. You may be perfectly justified in being angry if someone collides with your car and makes you late for an important meeting, but what good is your anger going to do? Unless you are constructively using your anger in a way that makes you feel good about yourself, being angry – no matter how justified – is pointless. More importantly, it's potentially damaging to you and to those you love. If your head is endlessly chuntering about the crimes and misdemeanours that you or your ex committed, or if you're punching at the air and screaming that the world's not fair, what good is this doing you? You may be 100 per cent justified, but it's getting you nowhere.

My Anger isn't Hurting Anyone

Wrong. It's definitely hurting you and almost certainly affecting others. Most of us have an inbuilt alarm system programmed to pick up anger signals from other people. As a society, it's important to know if someone near us is angry so we can keep a safe distance. Therefore, even if you think you're keeping your feelings well hidden, chances are those closest to you know you're angry and are not getting as close as you'd like. This can be particularly damaging for children who are relying on you for emotional support. As we saw earlier in this chapter, anger has significant negative consequences for the individual, keeping you trapped in the past and taking up valuable energy that could be used for creating a positive new future.

Being Angry is the Only Way I Can Get What I Want

There's a big difference between being angry and being assertive. Assertive behaviour is fair but persistent in ensuring justice is done, whereas anger intimidates and bullies others to comply with our wishes. However, anger often backfires. An angry approach is just as likely to antagonise your opponent and turn your situation into a battleground. You may have come from a background where you learnt that anger is the best way to get your needs met, but it's simply not true. If all you're interested in is revenge, then anger may be your best weapon, but if you want justice and fairness, then an assertive approach is far more likely to reap beneficial rewards.

If I Stop Being Angry, They'll Think I'm Okay with What Happened

In almost all situations, this simply isn't true. Our conscience is not activated or deactivated by anger. We know when something is right or wrong and when someone has been treated badly. Just because the victim handles the situation well, we don't doubt the seriousness of the crime; we marvel at the bravery and integrity of the victim. The other problem with this kind of thinking is that it offers no let-out in the future. If you're angry because your partner betrayed you, will you have to hang on to the anger all of your life to prove that it wasn't okay? Surely not. At some stage you will move on and your anger will fade and change. Does that mean it was okay? Of course not – it was still wrong but you've chosen not to be influenced by the offence for the rest of your life.

TRANSFORMING UNHEALTHY ANGER INTO HEALTHY ANGER

Managing your anger in a healthier and more productive way is all about changing your thought patterns. Generally speaking, thoughts precede emotions. We create our emotions from our thoughts. For example, if a man knocks into me in the street, I might think, 'That was stupid of him. He should have looked where he was going. He has no respect or regard for others. This is typical of what happens to me.' I am likely to feel angry if I think this way. However, if I think, 'I guess he's preoccupied with something and wasn't paying attention – accidents happen,' then I won't feel angry. If this sort of thing genuinely does happen to me on a regular basis, then I might think, 'These streets are too narrow and I'm tired of putting up with this. What's more, one day someone could get seriously hurt.' Then I might feel healthy anger and start a campaign for the council to pedestrianise the area.

The exercise opposite has been used by counsellors to help people identify negative thinking patterns and replace them with more positive ones. It's known as the ABCDE technique, originally designed by Albert Ellis, and you can use it to test each angry thought that you have. I've included an example opposite for your information.

You need to complete it starting with 1, the Consequence, which in this case will be anger. Then answer question 2, what triggered your anger, and 3, what was the thought behind this event. Question 4 challenges you to think of an alternative reason why the event may have happened, and finally, 5 gives you an indication of how changing your thinking might modify your anger.

A – Activating event (trigger)	*Ex doesn't reply to emails.*	2
B – Belief (thoughts, attitudes)	*He's deliberately being antagonistic. He's avoiding making important decisions about the divorce. He wants me to suffer for being the one who initiated the divorce.*	3
C – Consequence (emotion resulting from A+B)	*Anger.*	1
D – Dispute (question and generate alternative belief)	*Maybe his email account is on the blink. He's always been disorganised and slow to respond so this isn't really unusual. He may need more time to think before making a decision. He may be upset with me rather than angry.*	4
E – Effect of altering thoughts and beliefs	*I'll be more accepting of this being typical of him, rather than personal against me. I can have more compassion and be more generous about the timescale. I'll leave it a bit longer, then I'll telephone him and give him a nudge.*	5

As you can see from this example, brainstorming other reasons why someone or something has triggered your anger may help you to create a different meaning and therefore a different consequence and emotion. In the situation above, the anger may be triggered again if he still fails to reply, but by challenging and changing her thinking, she can continue to accept that neither her ex nor the situation is perfect. She can choose to remain in control and be assertive rather than become trapped by unhealthy anger and risk behaviours that will be counterproductive.

CHAPTER 6

Managing Doubt, Regret and Guilt

Perhaps one of the worst things about self-doubt, regret and guilt is that we tend to keep them to ourselves. We may talk about our grief, our fears and our anger – and seek the support and opinion of friends and family – but we often don't discuss the emotions that we hold ourselves accountable for. Doubt, regret and guilt tend to fester and grow alone. Without outsiders to challenge them, they can continue to be fed by our poor self-image and self-reproach.

Like all negative emotions, these are feelings that keep us stuck in the past. Change and growth are not possible until we can feel good about ourselves and positive about our future. Doubt and regret keep us trapped in a cycle of endless questioning, while guilt makes us wonder if we have any right to move on and be happy.

Some mistakenly think that these emotions are felt most strongly by those who leave their relationships, but the pain is often just as great for those who've been left. Whatever the circumstances of your break-up, there will be times when doubt makes you ask, 'Could I have done more?' If you struggle to answer the question adequately then regret will leave you saying, 'I wish I'd done more.' If left unabated, guilt will finally kick in and tell you, 'You should have done more.'

The best way to manage these feelings is to stop doubt in its tracks before it can escalate. In many cases, the doubts will be unfounded and based on exaggerated expectations of yourself. Other doubts may have been put there by other people, or because things have not gone to plan. Some doubts are inevitable. Any life-changing decision – even a positive one – is going to result in an occasional backwards glance, especially on the days when things aren't going as expected. For example, many people occasionally wonder if they chose the right career or the right home, and even the most in-love couple in the world will occasionally wonder if they made a mistake. Doubts are part of being human, of knowing that we're fallible.

If your partner is struggling to come to terms with the end of your relationship, or if you have children, you may feel the doubt more intensely. When others are affected by our decisions and behaviours, it's right that we should question ourselves, but not for ever and certainly not to the point where we tie ourselves in so many knots that we're unable to function.

There may be many doubts rushing around your head over the course of a separation. Some may be connected to a very specific event which triggered the end of the relationship, such as an argument or an affair, while others may be doubts about the whole relationship, such as, 'Should we have talked more?' But pretty much all of them boil down to the same doubt: 'Could I have done more to save my relationship?'

STOPPING DOUBT

Many counsellors use the zigzag technique to help people put a stop to their doubts. This is another creation of Albert Ellis. The principle of the zigzag technique is that you write down a positive belief that is the *opposite* of the doubt in the first box on the left, then challenge it in the box on the right, then defend on the left, and challenge again on the right. By repeating this process as many times as they need to, most people find they run out of arguments to support their doubt and give up on it. Below is an example of how one client, Tina, completed hers.

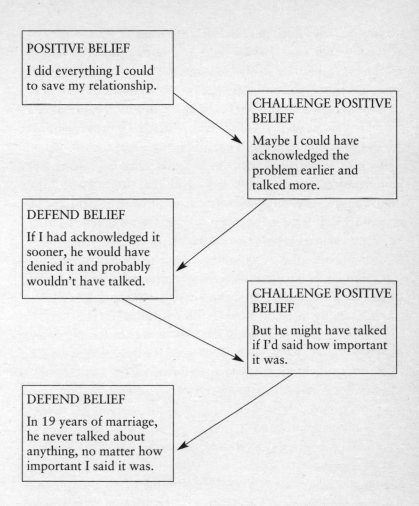

Take a piece of paper and write a positive belief, which is the opposite of your doubt, in the box on the left. Challenge that belief on the right, then defend on the left, then challenge on the right and so on. Fill in as many boxes as you need until you've confirmed your positive belief. If, however, your doubt is confirmed and you reach the decision that there were things you could or should have done to save your relationship, then you need to make a decision about how you handle those feelings.

DEALING WITH REGRET AND GUILT

Regret and guilt are similar in as much as they indicate that we made a mistake, though guilt carries the additional burden of a moral imperative. Regret tends to begin with 'I could have...' whereas guilt says 'I *should* have...' Whatever mistakes you've made, however, the reality remains that the decision to end your relationship has been made and it's final. At some point you must accept that what's done is done, and all the doubt, regret and guilt in the world won't change anything. You cannot change the past but you can choose whether to stay stuck in it or learn from it and move on.

Moving on means finding the grace to forgive yourself for the mistakes you made. Those mistakes may have been the result of a weakness, or because you simply didn't know any better at the time. Whatever the cause, it was a mistake. Humans make mistakes throughout their lives. Some are big, some are small, but all of them give us the opportunity to learn and become wiser and stronger as a result. But this can happen only if you make the decision to forgive yourself and move on.

Forgiving yourself won't just benefit you; it will benefit everyone around you too. In the same way that anger ties us to our ex and to our past, so do regret and guilt. When we let go of these negative emotions, we're also letting go of the past and freeing ourselves to focus on current and future needs – those of our family and friends as well as our own. Children, in particular, need their parents to heal from a broken relationship and move on, thereby giving them the security of knowing that a fulfilled and happy life can continue after divorce.

Take the time now to list the mistakes you made in your relationship that you want to forgive yourself for. Below is what Tina wrote:

I will forgive myself for:

Not recognising that there was a problem sooner
Not challenging him when his behaviour began to change
Being too absorbed in the children to do anything
Being too scared to talk to him about it
Not working harder earlier on in our relationship to learn to communicate better

Forgiveness is a long-term process. Unfortunately, it is common for our regrets and guilt to creep back up on us. When this happens, you can remind yourself that you're human and it's okay not to be perfect; that everyone makes mistakes but you've made the decision to learn and move on from yours, not be imprisoned by them.

Step Two may have been difficult for you. Learning to manage our emotions is an ongoing, life-long task. But for now, pat yourself on the back and get ready for Step Three.

Develop Strategies for Personal Growth and Support

Divorce is a personally challenging event, but one from which you can grow. This step will help you identify the many emotional and psychological strengths you already have, but may have forgotten about. Then we'll look at some of the personal struggles you may be facing or will have to face in the future, and end by developing an action plan for overcoming them.

CHAPTER 7

Identifying Your Emotional and Psychological Strengths

When a relationship breaks down, our self-esteem can take a massive bashing. Even the strongest and most resilient individuals have days when they wonder how they'll cope. However, unless you've spent all of your life living in some kind of space-age protective bubble, you will have already developed a host of coping tools and strategies. There'll also be a whole list of things you're good at, whether that's an actual skill like motor maintenance or accounting, or a character trait such as patience or friendliness. All of these things are resources that you can use to help you get back on your feet again after a divorce.

Unfortunately, it's very easy for us to forget our skills and natural resources, or take them for granted, especially when our self-esteem is low. If you've been in a conflictual or abusive relationship, or your partner left you with little explanation, then you may be feeling particularly bad about yourself. And if you struggled with low confidence before your relationship breakdown, it may be even harder to get back in touch with what you value about yourself.

THE IMPORTANCE OF POSITIVE SELF-ESTEEM

One dictionary defines self-esteem as: belief in oneself; self-respect. It could be further described as a sense of personal self-worth and competence; an awareness that you deserve a good and happy life and are capable of creating one.

In previous chapters we looked at how all humans are fallible and make mistakes. We also saw how we all sometimes struggle with negative emotions and have doubts and insecurities. The opposite is also true, however. We all have strengths and skills and experience positive emotions. We are all capable of great courage and great joy. A relationship breakdown tends to highlight our weaknesses and failings, but these other positive elements are nonetheless real. Getting back in touch with these things will help you not only to overcome the challenges and difficulties that you face, but also to realise your hopes and dreams for the future.

People with positive self-esteem tend to be happier, more successful and more creative, and have good relationships with other people. They believe that they are lovable and they look after themselves and other people. Because they're more confident, they tend to feel in control of their lives and are able to solve their problems and meet challenges when they occur. What's more, evidence suggests that people with positive self-esteem are both physically and mentally healthier and live longer lives. All of these benefits have a positive effect on those around them.

Our childhood and previous life experiences significantly influence our self-esteem. If you were brought up with criticism then you're more likely to have negative thoughts about yourself. If you were brought up with affirmations and praise, then you're likely to have a natural, inbuilt feeling of self-worth. The way we speak to ourselves is also something we begin to learn from our parents. If our inner voice is harsh and reprimanding, noticing only the times we did wrong or failed, then our self-esteem will drop. However, if our inner voice acknowledges and congratulates our efforts and successes, then our self-esteem increases.

Our self-esteem is mostly dependent on how we view ourselves and our world, but it's also influenced by our experience of how others view us and treat us. After our parents, our relationship with our partner is likely to have the biggest impact on how we feel. When we first fall in love we feel great. Our partner loves and cherishes every bit of us, warts and all. Over the years, however, this unconditional love and acceptance often changes. In later years, you may have lived with insults and put-downs that seriously eroded your self-esteem.

Some people find they get trapped in a bad relationship because, as their self-esteem becomes lower and lower, they no longer feel able to do anything to change their situation. Feelings of low self-worth can also leave you believing you'd never meet anyone better, and this relationship is as good as it'll ever get. If that describes how your marriage had become, then the good news is that now you're alone, you can rebuild and reclaim your self-esteem.

RECLAIMING YOUR SELF

Humans are complex beings, made up of many different facets. As we get into relationships with people, we tend to show the part of us that's most appropriate to that situation. For example, we show a different side of ourselves when we're out relaxing with friends than when we're playing with children or having a meeting at work. We may also unconsciously censor ourselves to show only the aspects that are accepted and encouraged by that other person, while other important qualities become suppressed.

This is particularly true in couple relationships. Over the years, there will have been some things about you that your partner didn't like, and some things that they were better at than you. These aspects of self often become hidden or even lost over the course of a relationship. For example, your partner may have been a better cook or had more patience than you, and consequently you've forgotten that these were also strengths of yours. Perhaps they were critical of your quiet self-containment, telling you that you were boring; or maybe they said that your gregariousness was loud and obtrusive. You may have lost touch with skills because you haven't needed to use them for a while, such as being good at budgeting or a good host. All of these hidden qualities can and will return if you commit to getting to know yourself again.

One way of getting to know ourselves and our positive qualities is to look at ourselves through the eyes of those who know us. You can do this by first listing all the different roles you play, especially the roles that involve other people. For example, Maria, a 48-year-old divorcée, wrote:

Roles I play:

Mum	*Daughter*	*Friend*
Sister	*Employee*	*Work colleague*
Volunteer	*Runner*	*Rug maker*

Many of us will have been brought up not to blow our own trumpet so it's difficult to list our good points. However, this can be easily overcome by putting yourself in the shoes of those you relate to and imagining what they would say if asked what they like and admire about you. So, once you've written your list of roles, you can begin to list the positive ways that you are viewed in them. Think also about the skills and personal attributes that you bring to each role. This is how Maria's looked:

> *Mum: Kids see me as loving, kind, generous, patient, good cook, also good at multi-tasking and managing conflict.*

Daughter: Parents see me as successful, thoughtful, a good mum, independent. Also good at choosing presents.

Friends: See me as a good listener, reliable, fun to be with and an optimist.

Sister: Brother sees me as a good listener, self-sacrificing, competent, resourceful and good host when they visit.

Work colleague: Colleagues see me as reliable, trustworthy, efficient and effective and a good laugh even when it's busy and stressful.

Employee: Boss sees me as reliable, responsible, good with figures and resourceful. Able to manage a challenge and not complain.

Volunteer: Others see me as faithful to the cause, dedicated and hard-working.

Runner: I'm dedicated and have got good stamina. Like a challenge.

Rug maker: Good with my hands, creative, good at following patterns and seeing good colour combinations.

You can use your notebook or get some paper to create your own list. Create two columns and head the first one 'Roles I play', and the second 'How I'm seen in this role, skills and character traits'.

Now you've done this, it's time to make those positive statements your own. When our self-esteem is low, it's tempting to add a 'yes, but...' to any compliment we receive. You might be saying to yourself right now: 'Yes, but my friends can't see me now,' or 'Yes, but my boss doesn't know me that well,' or 'Yes, but everyone can do that.' Minimising ourselves in this way may feel like a good thing to do. We may fear becoming cocky or arrogant, and think that being humble and self-effacing is better. Remember, though, that there's a big difference between being self-aware and being self-important. Knowing what you're good at is just as important as knowing what you're not good at. Both help you to become a mature, whole person. So, your next task is to summarise what you wrote above, preceded by 'I am...'

Once you've completed this exercise you should have a list of the things that you're good at and the personal character traits that make you good at these things. All of this can help you rebuild your confidence in yourself and in your ability to manage the future without your ex. Another way to increase that confidence is to remember the mountains you've already climbed and conquered.

PREVIOUS CONQUESTS

Few of us will have made it through life without some mountains, or at least molehills, to climb. Each time we conquer one of these challenges we become stronger and more resilient to future problems. The process of challenge also encourages us to dig deep into ourselves and discover new coping skills and strategies, and each subsequent event fine-tunes these abilities.

The challenges we face are different for all of us. Some may be losses you've experienced in the past, while others may be changes in lifestyle or career. You may have worked through health issues of your own or of someone you care for, or struggled with the difficult behaviour of others. Many ordinary and common life events also present us with a variety of challenges. These can include starting a family or moving home, or even just planning a significant holiday or family event or landscaping the garden. Then there are personal achievements that may be simple for someone else, but for us represented a major accomplishment. In each of these situations we will have called on our internal skills and resources to get us through.

Taking time to think about the things you've achieved and overcome can be another way of putting you in touch with your emotional and psychological strengths. Here's how Maria's list looked:

Previous Losses
Boyfriend dumped me at 23 after 4 years
Job redundancy
Grandma

Career Challenges
Retraining in sales and marketing
Doing the first major sales presentation

Life and Lifestyle Events
Having Ben and becoming a mum
Relocating to a different part of the country
Moving house
Rob's cancer scare
Having IBS

Personal Achievements
Running the London Marathon
Learning to sing

Once you've completed your list, go back through it and think about the personal qualities and strengths you drew on to help you meet each of these challenges. For example, Maria remembered that her confidence in her looks and her general optimism helped her to get over the break-up with her boyfriend at 23. Her success in managing many of life's changes was down to her ability to make friends easily and be pragmatic and efficient. Her dedication and stamina were positive character traits that helped her through almost everything that life had thrown at her.

You may find that going back over your 'I am...' statements will help you to create your personal qualities list. By the time you've completed the exercises in this section, you should be starting to realise that you already have many personal strengths and character traits that can help you with your divorce. Self-acceptance and self-knowledge are the keys to creating positive self-esteem. When you know and accept yourself you feel better and stronger, and when this happens your confidence and self-worth increases.

CHAPTER 8

Recognising Actual and Potential Personal Struggles

Everyone's experience of divorce is different. Consequently, each of us will be faced with very different personal struggles. Indeed, something that's a struggle for one person may be liberating for another. Being alone could bring freedom, space, an opportunity to go out and explore. For someone else, it may feel like an imprisonment, trapped alone in an insular world.

Perhaps one struggle that is common to most is the simple yet painful sensation of missing someone. If your break-up was particularly hostile then you may feel confident that you'll never miss your ex. Perhaps this is true, but there may well be times ahead when you will miss some of the things you did together, or just miss having another person around. Some people find that they miss being married and living with someone, even though they may not miss the actual person. Others miss a home they've left behind or children.

In Step Two we looked at the pain of grief and loss, and how these powerful emotions can be managed. Here, we're focusing more on the smaller struggles; the moments when you sigh and wish that things could have been different. This may not be of particular concern to you at the moment, but it's worth taking time to think about the challenges you may face in the future so you can be prepared for, or even pre-empt, them.

MISSING HAVING SOMEONE AROUND

If you've been living with someone, particularly if it's been for a long time, you'll probably have got used to having someone around: someone to say 'morning' and 'goodnight' to; someone to moan with about the weather or the morning's news headlines; someone who can pick up a pint of milk, chuck a load in the laundry or make sure the back door is locked. If you've got children it would also have been someone you could worry with if they were late home or running a temperature; celebrate with when they learnt a new word or did well at school; laugh with when they told a joke or did something funny.

Many things feel different when we're alone. The world becomes a quieter, more solitary place. Newly separated people often find they begin talking to themselves or having conversations with the cat. Not because they're going mad, but because they're so used to verbalising the events of the day. The home environment will be quieter too. No flushing of the loo, footsteps on the stairs or clattering of washing up. No one sighing, sneezing, coughing or snoring!

Along with the silence, there's often a physical sensation of there being too much space, for instance when sitting alone on the sofa, at the dining table or in the car. There's no passing in the hallway or bustling round the kettle at breakfast time or the sink at bedtime. A song popular in the seventies rang true for many people with its title – 'The Bed's Too Big Without You'. Suddenly even the smallest home can feel cavernous. These feelings can be particularly intense for those who have also left children behind. One client remembered:

> It was the silence that I found hardest to get used to. I'd often moaned at the boys for being so noisy, but after the novelty of being alone had worn off, I missed that noise

*so much. Saturday mornings were the worst. It had
always been a hectic time in the house. Now there was
just me wondering what the hell I'd do all weekend.*

Time can often feel different too. Some people find that they
have more time than they know what to do with. Things can
seem to take less time than they used to. Cooking, shopping
and cleaning for one take less time, and with no one to distract
you, chores are done quickly. Conversely, if you've got
children or had depended on your partner's practical support
in the past, you may find that you have a lot less time, and
you're working later into the evenings or having to get up
earlier just to get the basics done. For some, relaxation time
feels strange. Watching the television alone in the evening or
having a glass of wine doesn't quite feel right. Consequently,
some people find that they keep themselves busy because they
don't know how to switch off and unwind without someone
there to join them.

People often find particular times of the day or the week
difficult. For you, it could be mornings or evenings or the time
when you first get back from work. Or it could be weekends or
a certain day of the week when you'd previously always done
something together.

If any of this has left you sighing and thinking, 'That's me,'
or 'I can see how that could happen,' then stop reading and
take a moment now to jot down some of these actual or
potential challenges in your notebook.

MISSING CHILDREN

If you have children, then the time without them can feel
particularly painful. No one wants to leave their kids, but the
reality of divorce is that one or both of you may have long

stretches of time when you're not with them, while they're with the other parent.

As well as the noise and bustle of having them around, you may also miss some of your everyday routines. Some that may instantly come to mind are things like bath time and bedtime, reading stories or helping with homework, but there may be other little routines you never really noticed until they'd gone. For example, the way they always left their shoes in the middle of the hallway when they got in or never turned lights off after them; or the way they always mispronounced certain words or followed you round like a little shadow telling you about their day.

Physical touch and affection is also something we often take for granted within families. You may have got used to diminishing affection within your relationship with your partner and, like many, you may have found that you had become even closer to your children as a result. Children of all ages can be cuddly and loving, whether it's a small child climbing into your lap or a gangly teenager giving you a bear hug. Enjoying touch is an essential part of being human, and when it is taken away from you, even for a short time, it can feel like a physical wrench. You may find yourself compensating by grabbing a reluctant cat to stroke, hugging a cushion or developing a slightly embarrassing penchant for cuddly toys. Others make up for the lack of touch by getting more into the sensual pleasures of bath time and massage, or the simple delight of snuggling under a freshly washed duvet.

You may also miss the responsibility that goes with children. When there are others in your care, you have to think about what you're doing and the impact it will have on them. That includes the food you eat, the television you watch and whether or not you go out. Living alone can feel very odd as you can now do whatever you like, whenever you like, with no one to answer to. On some levels this can feel very freeing, but it can also be isolating. You don't have to 'care' for anyone, but similarly there's no one in your immediate vicinity who 'cares' for you.

MISSING YOUR HOME

Feeling homesick isn't something we often associate with divorce but since at least one person, if not both, has to leave the marital home, it's a very common side-effect. If you've built a home together, your house may have become what psychologists call a 'secure base', the place where you felt safe and at peace. The place that you retreated to in times of stress where you knew you could feel relaxed and recuperate ready to face the rest of life. When you lose that place, you lose your secure base, so it's really not surprising that you can feel disorientated, unsettled and unsafe. Thankfully, these feelings tend to be relatively short-lived, especially if you're able to quickly settle somewhere new. But if, like many, you've previously owned your home and have to move into rented accommodation, you may struggle to feel settled for some time. You may feel as if you're in temporary lodgings rather than a place you can call home, and as though you're stuck in limbo or living like a nomad.

Another thing that can contribute to feeling temporarily displaced and disorientated is the loss of familiar possessions – no longer having that picture above the fireplace, your coffee mug or comfy armchair, or sleeping in your own bed. The view from the window is different and the route to work has changed. On the surface these may seem fairly trivial losses, but when you're going through a stressful and emotional time, you need these home comforts even more. At the time when you need them most, for many, they're not there.

Take a few moments now before moving on to think about your home environment and the things that you may miss, and make a note of them.

EMOTIONAL STRUGGLES

People struggle with emotions other than grief, fear, anger, doubt and guilt (see Step Two). These may be temporary and fleeting, or they may become a bigger, more persistent problem. We'll start with the most common emotional struggle.

LONELINESS

There are many different depths of loneliness. At the shallow end you've got a nagging awareness of being alone, which can be alleviated by flicking on the television or radio. Then there's the sensation of loneliness that's akin to boredom and restlessness, moving from room to room or chore to chore, trying to keep busy, but knowing there's an emptiness that your activity can't fill. At the deep end there's the feeling of a gaping, hollow, endless expanse of loneliness, of being completely and hopelessly alone. Fortunately, most people never experience the really deep end of loneliness, or at least not more than briefly and occasionally. But many of us know it is there, and we skirt around the edges of that void, terrified of slipping in.

Loneliness is part of the human experience. We will all experience it at some level, at some time in our life. Some people are extroverts and need the company of others to feel at peace and experience life. Others are introverts, who are naturally more content in their own company. If you're the latter then loneliness may rarely crop up, or if it does, it won't be too intense. If, however, you're an extrovert by nature and you had always spent a lot of time with your ex, then the pain of loneliness may be more acute.

ISOLATION

Feeling isolated is not the same as feeling lonely, although both include the awareness of being alone. Loneliness is about needing company, needing to feel the presence of another human being alongside us. When this happens, we no longer feel alone. When we feel isolated, however, no amount of human company can alleviate the sensation of being alone. Isolation means feeling cut off and separated from other people, in spite of their presence.

Divorce can leave people feeling isolated for a number of different reasons. If no one among your family or friends has been separated, you may feel that those closest to you are unable to truly empathise with your situation. Alternatively, you may know or suspect that others won't be understanding about the reasons for your marriage breakdown. Or perhaps you're in a position where explaining the ins-and-outs of what went wrong is inappropriate. This can leave you feeling that you can share only part of your story, and the rest you must carry alone. Some people come from a family background where they've learnt to keep their thoughts and feelings private; consequently they may inadvertently isolate themselves from others through their silence.

One thing that is common to both loneliness and isolation is that, on the whole, they are a matter of choice. We can choose to reach out and connect more with other people, to reduce loneliness by spending time with others face to face or online, and to reduce isolation by sharing more of our story. It's not easy, especially if you've never needed to do it in the past, but in most circumstances, it is possible.

REJECTION

On the whole, rejection is felt most powerfully by those who have been left by a partner with little or no warning. However, rejection is also felt by many people who choose to initiate their divorce because their partner couldn't or wouldn't meet their emotional needs.

We feel rejected when someone chooses to turn away from us; when, in spite of our requests and desires, they say that they do not want to be with us but would prefer to be somewhere else or with someone else. Being rejected can leave us feeling that we're not worth being with, that we're unlovable. Rejection can be profoundly painful and leave us questioning whether it's just our ex who feels that way or if others feel the same.

Rejection can seriously damage our faith in ourselves and our faith in others. If we're not careful, it can cause us to limit our contact with others and result in loneliness and isolation. Some people cope with rejection by developing a hard shell that's impregnable to others' opinions. Logic says that if I don't care what others think then I can't be hurt or feel rejected again. However, this alienates others and can leave us feeling alone, struggling to form meaningful friendships and cynical of any future relationships.

If you're aware of feelings of rejection, then make a note of them now.

APATHY

This may not be an emotion that you would quickly associate with divorce; indeed, you may not think of it as an emotion at all. Perhaps that's because it feels okay. It's almost an absence of emotion, so there's nothing obviously negative about it. Unfortunately, however, the consequences of apathy can be devastating.

Divorce can be an exhausting experience. Some people cope by telling themselves they're not going to make any more effort in life because nothing really matters. People struggling with apathy may have lost their ambition and dreams for the future. They begin being late for things; they don't bother much about their health or appearance; and they become lazy about keeping in contact with friends and family. If you're finding yourself regularly saying, 'I can't be bothered,' then apathy is taking a hold and, if it's not dealt with, you may find yourself sinking into the pits of depression.

Before you move on, make sure you've listed in your notebook anything in this section that has rung a bell for you. Although it may not be a major issue now, if you've got any suspicion that it may become a problem in the future, it is important to deal with it now (see Chapter 9).

Your Action Plan

Divorce is difficult, stressful and challenging at best. For some it feels much worse – devastating and damaging. Whatever your experience may be, your divorce will herald a turning point in your life. Consequently, it provides you with an opportunity for personal growth and change.

In almost all situations, our emotions are governed by our thoughts. Therefore, if you change the way you think, then your emotions will change. Furthermore, once you've changed how you think, and therefore how you feel, then your behaviour will change. There are a few exceptions to this. Some emotions are instinctive ones over which we have no rational control. For example, if someone points a gun at you, you will instinctively feel fear; or if you accidentally put your hand into something slimy, you will feel disgust. Even in these situations, however, once our brain has kicked in and told us it's a toy gun or yummy honey, our feelings begin to change.

You may already be aware of this, but each of us has a little soundtrack inside our head that interprets a situation for us and tells us what to think – and what we think influences how we feel. The good news is that you are in control of that soundtrack. You can change the tune at any time you like and begin to listen to a more positive and happier voice. It often takes a bit of practice as the old voice will sometimes slip back on when you're not looking, but if you're determined enough, you can change the tape once and for all. With a new voice inside your head, you can begin to manage even the most painful emotions.

FURTHER STRATEGIES FOR DEALING WITH EMOTIONS

GRIEF AND FEAR

In Step Two you made a list of the things that you will miss now that your relationship is over. You also listed your fears and anxieties and rated them by probability, your power to avoid them, and their impact on your life. If you didn't complete these exercises at the time, then you can go back and do them now.

Looking at the things that you'll miss, how many of them can, in time, be either replaced by something or someone else or restored? Which things do you think that, in time, you'll get so used to being without that it won't matter any more?

In Step Two we looked at Alan's list of the things he would miss about his marriage (see page 43). When he worked through his list, he saw that certain things would probably be replaced fairly soon. For example, by meeting someone else or spending more time with friends, he was less likely to miss his wife's advice and support, and having someone to relax with in the evening and go on holiday with. He felt that his security of being known and understood, and his attachment to his home, would be restored over time. Although he felt displaced and estranged in his flat, he decided that these were temporary emotions. He could contentedly learn to live without his in-laws, having dinner cooked for him and someone to talk to when he got home. This left him with missing the children. He suspected that he would get used to seeing them less, and he also decided that he wanted to create a more positive action plan for seeing them more often. Ultimately, however, he had to accept that this would always be a source of pain.

Working through your list of things you'll miss in this way gives you the opportunity to write a new soundtrack for your inner voice. When you hear it saying, 'I'm really missing…' you can add 'but I know in time it will be replaced, restored or matter less'. Inevitably, there will always be some things that are painful, but even if you can't rewrite this script, you can edit it. For example, Alan learnt that although he couldn't stop his inner voice saying 'I miss my boys,' he began to add 'but I'm so lucky to have them and I will make the most of every chance I have to see them'. The pain was still there, but he was able to balance it with positive thoughts.

This same technique can be especially powerful for over-coming fears and anxieties. Looking back at the list you created in Step Two, pick out the ones that rated high in probability, low in power to avoid, and high in impact. Ideally, your thinking will have already begun to change on the fears that you realise are highly improbable and the ones you feel you can avoid, but think now about how you can manage the bigger fears and anxieties. Sometimes looking at the worst-case scenario is the best way to help you think more positively. I know that sounds illogical, but if you can squarely look in the face of your fear, then you can begin to plan what you'd do about it if the worst should happen. For example, Alan was particularly worried about losing his job and how he'd manage financially, so he began to explore what he'd do if it happened. He thought about how he'd look for another job or set up his own business. If that failed, he considered what it would be like to live on benefits for a while. It wasn't a particularly pleasant thought, but with the loving support of family and friends around him, he knew he'd cope well enough until another job turned up.

ANGER AND RESENTMENT

If, after completing the ABCDE exercise on page 57 on your angry thoughts, you realise that some of your anger is healthy and justified, you may decide that you want to set yourself some goals to overcome this situation. For example, you might decide that you want to change contact arrangements with your children or be more assertive with your ex over a financial decision. (For more on setting goals, see Step Seven.)

If there have been events in your marriage that have left you with strong feelings of anger or resentment, the only way to completely free yourself may be to make the decision to let it go. It can be difficult to let go of a powerful emotion as it can feel as though you're letting an ex get away with it, but harbouring anger will ultimately damage you, not them. Letting go of anger is not a one-off event; it's a process that can take many years. Some people have found it helpful to write down their angry thoughts and then symbolically dispose of them – either burning them on a fire, throwing them in the bin, or even flushing them down the toilet. You may have to do this on a number of occasions before the feelings begin to subside, but eventually, with time and effort, you can be free of them.

DOUBT, REGRET AND GUILT

As we saw in Chapter 6, the key to overcoming doubts, regret and guilt is self-forgiveness. If, after completing the zigzag exercise (see page 61), you're unable to reassure yourself that you did everything you possibly could, then you need to make a decision to forgive yourself for making a mistake and not being perfect. Like many people, you may not have too much difficulty forgiving others when they've made a mistake, but it may take some time for you to be able to truly forgive yourself.

One way to help this process is to make a positive decision to learn from your mistake or weakness, or whatever you feel your failing was, so that you can be confident it won't happen again. For example, if you feel that you could or should have communicated more or learnt to manage conflict better, then you may decide to set a goal of learning more about this and improving your skills. If you're feeling guilty about an affair or regret staying in a relationship with an unfaithful partner for so long, then you may decide to read up on affairs and try to understand your behaviour better. (For more on setting goals, see Step Seven.)

LONELINESS AND ISOLATION

The best way to overcome loneliness and isolation is to spend more time connecting with other people (for more on this, see Chapter 10). No matter how many friends you have and how close you are, however, there may still be times when you feel lonely or isolated. On the occasions when your feelings cannot be alleviated by getting in touch with someone else, then how you interpret these lonely sensations will make all the difference between experiencing them as a minor discomfort and feeling overwhelmed by them. It all goes back to that inner voice. If, when you feel lonely, your soundtrack says, 'You're all alone, nobody loves you, nobody cares about you,' then you're going to feel sad and even lonelier. However, the feelings will be more manageable if you say to yourself, 'It's understandable that I feel lonely now because I'm alone, but these feelings will subside and tomorrow I can phone someone or go out and spend time with people and feel connected again.'

If you're in a crowded place and find yourself feeling isolated, you can either listen to the soundtrack that says 'You're all alone, no one here knows what you're going through, no one understands' and consequently feel worse; or you can change the tape to 'There are probably lots of people here who've been through similar experiences to me and I have much more in common with them than I realise', and then you'll begin to feel better. As your feelings are influenced by your thoughts, changing your thought process to recognise that the feeling is temporary and natural will make the emotion begin to lose its power and subside.

REJECTION

The same technique of changing the soundtrack is also true for managing feelings of rejection. This is only part of the story, though, because with rejection often come powerful feelings of low self-esteem. In Chapter 7 we looked at the importance of positive self-esteem and how seeing yourself through the eyes of those who love you can help you have a more complete and realistic view of yourself. We also explored the previous challenges you may have faced in your life, and how the strengths and character traits that got you through those events can help you now. Positive self-esteem is based on self-acceptance and self-knowledge. Just because one person has decided not to love you does not mean that you're unlovable. If you wrote down a list of positive statements earlier, you may find it useful to rewrite this list on something that you can keep with you for when feelings of rejection strike. If you want to do more work on your self-esteem, then you may want to have that as one of your goals for personal growth. For example, you may decide that your self-esteem would improve if you were more assertive or optimistic. Or perhaps you need to become more confident in a particular area of your life, such as within friendships or at work. For some, improving self-esteem means working with a counsellor to look back at negative childhood messages and re-write them.

APATHY AND MOTIVATION

Apathy is one of the biggest obstacles to overcoming any problem – feeling that it's just not worth it and you can't be bothered. Beneath this apathy is sometimes a deeper fear that change just isn't possible, or the effort required to change won't justify the end result. Basically, this all boils down to motivation but, contrary to popular belief, motivation isn't something that spontaneously erupts in some people and not others. It's a state of mind and a feeling of purpose that can be created. Motivation may come from outside – for example by focusing on the benefits of change for your family, friends or career – or it can come from inside, a personal desire to get better and be better.

It's worth being aware that feelings of motivation will often go up and down. There will be days when you feel inspired and energised, and days when you feel indifferent and hopeless. Whatever you do, however, don't wait for an 'up day' before you begin to make changes and work on your goals. Success builds motivation faster than anything else, so the sooner you make a start, the faster your motivation will grow and you'll reach your goals. On the days when your motivation is low, you may find the following tips helpful:

➤ Remember why you're doing this. Focus on all the benefits – both emotional and practical – for yourself and others around you. Think, also, about the consequences of doing nothing, of staying the same. Is that something you want to live with for the rest of your life?

➤ Be inspired. Think about the people in your life or in stories that you've read who have successfully turned round something in their life. People who have been successful in either little or big ways, whether it's a family member, a friend or a celebrity or character in a film. All these people can be role models for you.

➤ List previous successes. There will undoubtedly have been times in your past when you set yourself goals and achieved them. Whether that was passing an exam, mastering a skill, overcoming a phobia or becoming better at something, you have successfully changed before and you can do it again.

➤ Record your progress. Make sure you review your goals regularly. Not only will this help you to stay on track, but seeing that change is happening – however slowly – will encourage you to continue with your goals.

➤ Have some handy quotes. Self-help books, films, television programmes, celebrities and family and friends can all offer you words of wisdom for your hour of need. Make a note of anything that particularly resonates with you and keep it handy.

SETTING GOALS

If you want to be sure that you're moving forward and not backward, then setting goals for what you want to achieve is an excellent first step. Many people don't reach their goals in life because they're too vague and often too big. For example, if you set a goal of 'I want to be happy', you're almost certainly going to fail, at least some of the time. Not only is it unrealistic, but what we perceive as happiness changes on a regular basis. To 'be happy' is a nice aspiration, but it's not really a goal. In the excellent book *Cognitive Behavioural Therapy for Dummies*, the authors recommend that all goals should follow the SPORT acronym:

Specific: Make your goal as specific as you possibly can. Think about how you want to feel, think and act differently and in what situations. For example, rather than saying, 'I want to feel more relaxed,' you might say, 'I want to feel more relaxed and chat more freely with friends.'

Positive: State your goal as a positive rather than a negative. So rather than saying, 'I want to feel less angry/fearful,' you'd say that you want to feel calmer or more confident. You should be aiming to move towards a positive feeling state rather than running away from a negative one.

Observable: Try to include in your goal something that makes it measurable from a behavioural viewpoint so you'll know when you're being successful. So as well as your goal saying, 'I want to be more comfortable in my own company,' you might also add 'and fidget less'.

Realistic: Make sure your goals are realistic and achievable. It's much better to have 10 small goals that you can reach than one big one that you can barely achieve. If you're still in a lot of pain about your divorce, then saying 'I want to feel happy about the end of my marriage' may be unrealistic, at least for now, so saying 'I would like to feel healthy, manageable sadness' is much more realistic and appropriate.

Time: Set a time frame to work within. If you have no time limit at all then it can be hard to measure your success, though be sure you don't set yourself up to fail by giving yourself an unrealistic deadline. Think, also, if your goal may be quantifiable in terms of the number of times it happens. For example, you may set a goal of spending a certain amount of time per week with the children, or limiting your negative thinking to a maximum of 10 minutes a day.

Below are some examples of SPORT goals that clients set to help them in their personal growth and survival following a divorce.

To become calmer and more relaxed about the suddenness of Bill's departure by reminding myself that I am okay and I am coping, and that the suddenness was his responsibility, not mine. I would like to achieve this over the next three months, consequently reducing my physical symptoms of anxiety and enabling me to start sleeping better.

To become more patient with the children by snapping at them less and generally enjoying their company more. To do this I will work on reducing my anger with my ex by improving my communication skills. I'd like to get better at this before Christmas.

I want to feel more comfortable and confident in my own company and less fidgety by finding new things that I can enjoy doing alone.

To understand why I had an affair by reading up on the subject more, and being more open with friends I trust to challenge and care for me. I want to achieve this before I consider getting into another long-term relationship.

To become better at managing conflict, not just in relationships but also with family and friends. I'll achieve this by seeing a counsellor and reading self-help books. Hopefully, I can feel more confident about this by the end of the year when we'll be due in court.

To work on raising my self-esteem by reading more on the subject and spending more time with people who make me feel good about myself. I will read a book by the end of the month and see people who make me feel good at least twice a week.

Take some time now to look back over this section and write down any goals that will help you to manage your emotions better. Remember to follow the SPORT guidelines whenever you can and review your goals regularly.

Make the Most of Family and Friends

We often don't realise just how many friends we have until we take the time to count them. This step is about the friends, family and other support networks that you can call on in your hours of need. We'll start by looking at who's already there for you and then explore the stresses that separation can put on children, extended family and friendships. The final chapter in this step will help you to create an action plan for extending your social groups and deepening existing friendships.

CHAPTER 10

Identifying the People Who are
There for You

The fear of loneliness and isolation is common to pretty much everyone during a relationship break-up. Even those people who leave one relationship to go straight to another fear that the circumstances of the break-up may alienate them from some friends; and with the new relationship still in its infancy, there are often significant, if unspoken, anxieties that it won't last.

The stigma of divorce can leave us feeling cut off from people, but this is often an emotional response rather than a practical fact. It's certainly true that when times are hard, we discover who our real friends are. A few of us may find that we don't have as many friends as we'd like, and that perhaps we've neglected some friendships. While there are very few people who have no friends or family, sometimes families drift apart, often due to geographic distance or employment needs. Opening your eyes to the family, friends and communities around you will not only reduce feelings of isolation, but also give you additional confidence to face challenges.

FAMILY SUPPORT

Nowadays, families come in many different shapes and sizes. You may have parents, step-parents, grandparents, step-grandparents, siblings, half-siblings, step-siblings, aunts, uncles, cousins, nieces, nephews and a whole load of other relations.

You may also have grown up with people who were like family; perhaps you even called them family names, even though you weren't related at all. All of these people can provide, to a lesser or greater degree, family support.

If you experienced marriage breakdown in your childhood, then you may be tempted to blame your current situation on your background. If you choose to do this, you can reframe your thoughts more positively. Although you didn't grow up with a good model of what a healthy relationship should be like, at least you should be well trained in what a relationship *shouldn't* be like. You may also have more people in your family who have had first-hand experience of what you're going through. Everyone's relationship and separation is different, but we can learn just as much from those whose attitudes differ from ours as from those who share our views. Some people bemoan the loss of the traditional core family, but the great thing that second families provide is access to a wider range of people and experiences. With that come wider opportunities to build positive, rewarding family relationships.

Perhaps the reason that many people turn to their family in crisis is because of the history that you share, and because family members often know different sides of us than friends or colleagues do. Your mum can remember with a smile that since you were a little girl you were stubborn and always fought for what you wanted. A dad may remind his son that he was always popular at school and had to fight off the attention of wannabe girlfriends. Family can also see through the defences that we try to put up, and instinctively know that when we say we're okay, what we really need is a hug. Siblings are often the same. Even if you have little in common on a day-to-day basis, there's often an emotional connection that runs deep.

Some people worry about turning to family in times of crisis because they don't want to worry anyone. Or your concern might be that your family will interfere or say, 'I told you so.' All of this may be true in part. Parents will inevitably worry about you – it's part of their job – and if they never really approved of your choice of partner, they may not be surprised that it didn't work out. Remember, though, that you're an adult now and your family may have changed. Even if they haven't, there may still be practical ways that they can support you. Family members can help you through a divorce in so many different ways.

FRIENDS INDEED

A friend in need is a friend indeed, or so the saying goes. So now, in your hour of need, it's time to count up your true friends. Remember that friendships fulfil many different functions. It's unlikely that any single person could ever fulfil all of your needs, and that's true of partners as well, but each friendship can provide some things of importance. Friendships fall into categories like this:

BEST MATES

This is the person, or if you're lucky, a few people, who you generally feel closest to. You probably know each other very well and feel in tune with each other. You may see a lot of each other or you may not. Closeness and contact are not the same thing. You may sit next to the same person at work every day and not feel even remotely close to them, but only see a best friend two or three times a year. What measures a best friend is how quickly you fall back into step with them, even when the absences have been long.

Best mates are honest with each other. They will challenge or even risk hurting you if they feel it's in your best interests. They'll keep your confidences and put themselves out for you whenever it's humanly possible. With best mates, there's mutual trust, mutual respect and mutual care, but that doesn't mean it will always be at the same time. The nature of any relationship is that sometimes one person is more needy than the other. You may have leant on a best mate more than they've ever leant on you, or perhaps you've always been in the supporting role, but best friends know that they can rely on each other whenever circumstances mean the roles reverse.

FUNCTIONAL FRIENDS

These friends tend to play a particular role in your life. You both like each other and you'll probably want to help each other out if you possibly can, but neither of you would describe yourselves as particularly close. You may share a common interest, such as a sport or hobby, being parents or living on the same street, or you may have particular skills that you reciprocate with each other, such as having a plumbing friend or computer mate. Your relationship may work on the basis of swapping favours as well as swapping a laugh. Or your commonality may be based on another mutual friend – for example, your partners may be friends with each other.

Functional friends often spend time with each other when they're needed or in the mood. They're the social buddy or someone who can lift your mood and help you get lost in another activity when you need to. These are recreational relationships which may develop into a deeper friendship, or may continue as they are for many, many years.

CASUAL ACQUAINTANCES

These are people you work with and friends of friends. If you were throwing a big party you'd invite them to make up the numbers. That's not to say that you don't value them or like them, because you do; but if you're really honest, they are the group of friends that can drift in and out of your life with little consequence. There may also be people in this group that you would really like to get to know better. You may suspect that you would become good friends if the circumstances were right, but perhaps because of time, geographic distance or office politics, they remain a warm smile and a handshake away.

CREATE A FRIENDSHIP MAP

Friendships often evolve and change over the years, and different life events bring people closer or create more distance. You may have lost touch with some friends almost completely because of the demands of your relationship or due to the nature of the break-down, but you may find they're not as far away as you think.

One way of exploring how close you feel to members of your family and friends is to complete what therapists call intimacy circles. By using a diagram of concentric circles, putting yourself in the middle, you can then map friends and family to see how close they are to you. Here's how one person's looked:

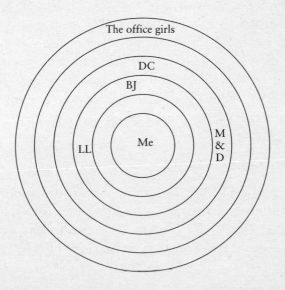

Now complete your own intimacy circle. Remember to put family members on as well and all the different types of friends that you have.

OTHER SOCIAL GROUPS

On the whole, humans are social beings. It seems to be part of our nature to form family groups and communities. In olden days, those would have centred on where we lived, but now our communities might also be based around workplaces or leisure activities.

Many of us seriously underestimate the number of other social groups of which we're a part. It's easy to become insular and just see the people immediately around us, but beyond that are countless others. All of these groups can be a resource for you, either to build further friendships and relationships or to call on for practical advice and support. With your intimacy circle you've already created your own world. Now visualise your further friendship groups as other planets orbiting around the circle. Add these satellites to your intimacy circle. You may find that going back to notes you wrote on the roles you play will help to jog your memory. Here's an example to get you thinking more:

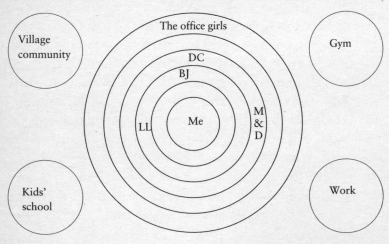

Now that you have a map of all the people close to you in your world, and all those orbiting around the edges, you can work out how these family, friends and other social groups can support you best.

RECOGNISING OUR NEEDS

All human beings have basic emotional and psychological needs. Depending on your character and your life experience, you will need different things in different measure; and there will be certain times in your life when you need some things more than others. For example, if you've just lost your job then your need to feel respected, successful and valued may be higher than normal. If you've just moved into a new neighbourhood, you may need to be acknowledged, recognised and included more than you did before. The truth is that we're often unaware of our needs until they're not being met. Then, suddenly, we may find that we have a gaping emotional hole.

Our spouse or partner will, to a greater or lesser degree, have fulfilled many of our emotional needs. Now that you're alone, you will need to turn to yourself and to others for these needs to be met. It can feel uncomfortable to be emotionally needy, but remember this is a temporary and totally normal reaction to divorce. Once you're back on your feet again, you won't need to be so dependent on friends. However, as you'll see in Chapter 12, one welcome side-effect of divorce is that friendships often deepen, families become closer and individuals get more involved in their communities. Turning to others in a time of need is what friendship is all about.

Below is a list of common emotional and psychological needs. Take the opportunity to tick the needs that are important to you, adding any more that come to mind. Then, turn to your completed intimacy circles and satellites and note the name of each person or group who may be able to help you meet that need.

Common Emotional and Psychological Needs

To be accepted
To be acknowledged
To be appreciated
To feel capable
To feel competent
To be happy
To feel heard
To feel important
To be included
To be loved
To be needed
To feel optimistic
To feel reassured
To be recognised
To be respected
To feel safe
To feel successful
To be able to switch off
To be understood
To be useful
To be valued

You may find that there are a few surprises. When we really look at who our friends, family and social groups are and what they provide for us, we can begin to see just how many of our needs can be met. Some friends may not be very good at understanding you or making you feel heard, but they may be great for cheering you up and helping you to look on the bright side. Some family members are great for making you feel safe and loved, even if they're useless at doing anything practical to help. Like you, the people in your life have different gifts and qualities. Knowing who's there for you when you need them, and which of your needs they are able to meet, is undoubtedly one of the most valuable resources you have.

CHAPTER 11

Recognising Challenges in Family and Social Relationships

You'll never know how much your marriage affects other people until you get divorced. Until now, you may have been under the illusion that how you conducted your personal life within the confines of your home was no one else's business. As you'll soon discover, however, divorce is a very public affair and it affects more people than you could have ever imagined.

YOUR CHILDREN

First and foremost are your children. There are few people nowadays who are totally unaware of the impact of divorce on children, but it's worth taking some time to explore the scope of that impact so you can be ready for the fallout.

Children of all ages are affected by divorce. A baby or small child who may be too young to understand what's going on can still pick up on a parent's distress; they may regress to an earlier developmental stage such as taking longer to settle, needing a bottle or bedwetting. Children between the ages of five and eight will have more understanding of the situation and be easier to comfort with words, but this age group can be particularly sensitive to separation from a parent, and may become very fearful of losing a parent for ever. Children between nine and 12 are the group most likely to respond with anger as they feel acutely aware of the injustice of the situation that is being forced on them. The 13-plus group, who are generally more understanding of the complexities of relationships and the imperfections of the world, have their own roller coaster of adolescent emotions to contend with as well.

Common to all children will be feelings of loss, sadness, confusion, frustration and anger. Many will demand answers to their incessant 'why' questions to try and get more understanding and control of the situation. All will be susceptible to taking sides in order to try to redress what they may see as inequality and unfairness, especially if they are receiving negative messages about the other parent. A frightening number of children blame themselves for their parents' divorce.

The effects of divorce and separation on children can be far-reaching. Evidence shows that children from separated families may struggle more at school and have behavioural and relationship problems. Don't lose hope, however, because evidence also shows that it is the conflict surrounding divorce and the quality of contact with both parents that makes the difference, not the actual event of divorce itself. So by avoiding conflict and ensuring regular contact with both of you, you can minimise the impact. What's more, follow-up studies of the children of divorce show that most do adapt to the changes and are happy with their lives.

It's important to remember that divorce is something that affects children's lives for ever. It is not an event to be 'got through'; it is a permanent change to their family structure. As well as the emotional upheaval of discovering your parents no longer love each other and one of them is leaving, there are also the practical changes that they have to endure. For many there is less money, and perhaps a new home, new school and a new timetable of juggling two parents and two homes. This is a time when your children need you to be strong and there for them, but this coincides with the toughest time in many parents' lives when they feel they have the least emotional and practical resources to provide for their children. While you're trying to pick up the pieces of your own life, and perhaps your heart as well, your children need you to be the best parent that you can be. Parenting through divorce is perhaps the toughest challenge you'll ever face. For more on parenting, see Chapter 16, and the Relate guide entitled *Help Your Children Cope with Your Divorce* (see Further Reading).

YOUR EX'S FAMILY

Another family consideration is your ex's relatives. If you've always been close to their family, and especially if you have children who create an ongoing biological bond, you'll need to think about how you'll continue to relate to them. The questions you need to ask yourself are: Do you like them? Do they like you? Do you need them? Do they need you? If you have children then the bigger question is: Do your children need them? Unless there's a safety reason why your children shouldn't see your ex's family, then the answer is 'yes'. However, that doesn't necessarily mean that you'll be involved in maintaining contact.

If you've enjoyed a good relationship with members of your ex's family in the past, a relationship that has been independent of the common denominator of your ex, then you'll probably want to try and stay in touch. If your divorce has been acrimonious then it may be wise to let the dust settle for a while; but once life is getting back on an even keel for both you and your ex, you may want to get back in touch. Be warned, though: divorce has a tendency to create rifts in which each person feels they must take a side. If you have been perceived to have been in the wrong or hurtful in any way to your ex, then their family may decide that, out of loyalty, they should have nothing more to do with you. This can be a very painful experience, particularly if you had felt close to them or had become dependent on them for practical support, but unfortunately this is often the reality of divorce.

In the majority of cases, what tends to happen is that families slowly separate. You may find that without your ex in the picture, you have very little in common with the in-laws. Beyond the required politeness and civility of passing in the street or perhaps meeting at a bigger family gathering, you gradually drift apart. In some instances, the decision is not mutual, and you may find yourself wanting to maintain some relationships while getting the distinct impression that they're trying to give you the heave-ho. Or you may be surprised to find a member of your ex's family desperately trying to stay close to you when you'd prefer to let the distance grow.

YOUR EX'S FRIENDS

In the same way as you may have become close to your ex's family, there may be friends of theirs you've become particularly fond of, people with whom you'd like to stay in touch. Conversely, you may be relieved to think that you'll never have to endure another dull moment with your ex's work colleagues or old school friends again. There may be other friends you've become very close to in your own right or, like many couples, you may have become close to your ex's friend's partner. This can cause a whole load of extra problems and complications, as one client, Zoë, recalled:

> My ex, Pete, had been best mates with Nick since college days, and over the years I got really close to his wife, Kate, especially after our children were born and went to the same school. Pete and I split up after his second affair but Nick thought I should have stood by him and given him another chance, and decided that he didn't want

anything else to do with me. Kate was much more understanding and sympathetic but Nick gave her such a hard time every time she saw me that in the end she gave up. She said she didn't want to ruin her marriage because of mine. I realise that she was in an impossible situation, but I can't help feeling really angry and let down.

Zoë was particularly unlucky, but situations like this are not uncommon after a divorce. Spend some time thinking about your current and future relationships with your ex's family and friends. Are there any that may become complicated or that might provide challenges in the future?

YOUR EX AS A FRIEND

A few couples manage to negotiate a transition from partners to friends very easily. Many couples don't even want to try. As with most things in a relationship, there is little right or wrong. Some people feel very strongly that they want to 'stay friends', and sometimes this masks a reluctance to acknowledge the end of the relationship. Saying 'but we can still be friends' softens the blow and takes away the finality of divorce. While continuing to be 'friendly', especially if you've got children, is a good thing, remaining friends may not be. First, friendship is based on equality, on being able to give and take in equal measure, emotionally and practically. Often when couples attempt to stay friends, it becomes obvious that one is still more emotionally involved than the other. Another problem can arise when new relationships come on the scene and old feelings of jealousy and hurt are rekindled.

If you and your ex can reach a place where you can be mutually supportive and caring while encouraging each other's autonomy, then good on you. Be aware, though, that there can be many pitfalls and hazards en route to this kind of relationship, and you may sometimes be the casualty.

YOUR FRIENDS

You may think that your friendship groups won't be affected by your divorce, but they undoubtedly will. Many people find that their friendships deepen as they share more about the personal difficulties they're experiencing, and friends respond by being more open about their lives. Unfortunately, this is not true of all friendships. Some people will disapprove of your divorce. They may feel strongly that you should have done something differently and begin to withdraw from the friendship, either openly or subtly. If this happens then you may decide that since they can't support you, you'd prefer not to be friends anyway. This can still be painful, however, as someone you had once valued has made a moral judgement on you.

There may be other friends who find your divorce threatening and destabilising of their status quo. They may have hidden issues in their relationship that your situation has highlighted, issues that they would rather not confront. Having your story in their lives may be too close for comfort; consequently they may try to distance you physically or make sure your conversations always remain on comfortable ground.

FACING SOCIAL STIGMA

With divorce being so commonplace nowadays, it can be hard to believe that there is still any stigma attached. However, anyone who's divorced can list a number of times when they've felt like an outsider or even an outcast because of their change of marital status.

The first one you may confront is completing forms. When asked for your status you must choose between separated or divorced. The single and married options are no longer available to you. For many people, this can feel like an intrusion on their privacy at best, and at worst, a demand for a public declaration of their inability to make their relationship work. From a legal perspective, you do not go from married back to single; you go from married to failed married.

Other public situations include works dinners, school plays or parents' evenings, community events and even shopping. When you're newly single it can feel as if you've suddenly been transported into a world that consists only of couples and perfect 2.4 families. While this isn't true, many people do feel as if their singleness makes them stick out like a sore thumb.

Another impact can be on your social life. If many of your friends are couples you may find yourself no longer being invited to quite so many dinner parties. For some reason, some hosts can get very flustered about there being an odd number around the table. When you're invited to a larger social function, you may find your invitation includes that ominous line '… and friend'. This is great if you have a friend to take, but if not, it's easy to worry that it's not okay to go alone. At times it may feel as though being single is a bigger problem for some of your friends than it is for you. As a result, you may find yourself swinging between giving heartfelt reassurances that you really are okay and acute embarrassment that you're alone. Or you may decide to spare everyone's feelings and hide your new status by staying at home!

Before moving on to the next chapter, make sure you've made a note of everything that may cause issues for you, and then we'll look at how to overcome them in the next chapter.

CHAPTER 12

Your Action Plan

When you go through any kind of crisis you quickly find out who your real friends are and who you want to be your real friends. As the weeks and months unfold after separation, you will probably receive numerous texts, phone calls and visits; offers of a shoulder to cry on, a night out on the town or practical help with the challenges of living alone. Some of these offers may come from unexpected places; and others, who you thought would be there for you, aren't.

It's also a time when we may re-evaluate friendships for ourselves. The shoulder to cry on may not be as comfortable as you thought, and the promised fun night out may have been miserable. You may begin to discover that you don't want to be as close to some people as you thought, while others with whom you may have had a rather superficial relationship turn out to be soul mates. You may also get closer to some family members. Parents or a brother or sister may show a side of themselves that you hadn't previously seen, and you may begin to enjoy a different sort of relationship.

All of these are natural changes that often occur after a divorce. Many will be pleasant and welcome, though a few may be less so. As well as these natural changes, however, you can choose to be proactive in your relationships; to build new friendships and deepen some that already exist.

MAPPING HOW YOU'D LIKE YOUR FRIENDSHIPS TO BE

Look back at the intimacy circle you completed in Chapter 10. I'd like to invite you to map out how you would like your friendship diagram to look. Draw some more concentric circles. As you begin to complete your intimacy circle, consider if there are people you would like to be closer to you. Are there any who are fine where they are now? Are there some you'd prefer to be further away? Remember to include family members you're close to as well. Are there people in your satellite circles you would like to get to know better and draw into your inner map?

Here's how Yolanda's looked.

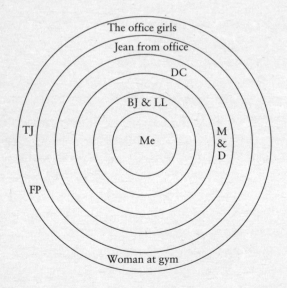

Yolanda wanted to have some friends closer and also decided that there were a few people in her satellites that she wanted to get to know. A couple of them were other single mums from her children's school, and another was a woman at work who she'd always been able to have a really good laugh with. There were also a couple of people who were often at the gym at the same time as her who she thought it would be nice to chat to.

Once you've completed your intimacy circle, you'll have a good overall picture of the relationships you want to maintain, the ones you want to deepen, and those you want to create.

NURTURING FRIENDSHIPS

You may have many friendships that you're basically happy with, but perhaps you have discovered that you need to work a little harder at maintaining them. Most of us are guilty of taking our friendships for granted. When we're busy with work or family life, our friendships can slip down our priority list. You may also have fallen into the pattern where it was always your friend that contacted you, and although you always enjoyed seeing them, you almost never initiated contact. Well, now is the opportunity to get better at making and maintaining contact.

In Chapter 8 we talked about loneliness and isolation, and you may have recognised that there are particular times of the day or week when you struggle most with this. The evenings may be hardest for you, or weekends, or during the day when the kids are at school. Each of these times presents a perfect opportunity to phone a friend. Better still, make a regular arrangement to meet. You may find it helpful now to make a list of your friends and a list of the times when you struggle most and check who's available. There may be a few people you could call or arrange to see at certain times but few or none at others because of their commitments to work or family. If this is the case, then make a note to yourself to expand your friendships to include people who are also available when you need them.

We looked at our basic emotional and psychological needs in Chapter 10, and you wrote a list of which friends met which needs. Now you can think about matching up your low points with the friends that are available and the particular needs you'd like to be met. For example, Yolanda recognised that her low points tended to be weekday evenings when she'd put the kids to bed. She was mostly busy during the day and was fairly successful at making plans for the weekend, but from 7pm on Mondays to Thursdays, she often got quite low. She noted down a number of friends who were available to chat on the phone or over the internet or available to meet up. Beside these names, she wrote what these friends were particularly good at:

> LL – *pretty good at everything, but particularly good at being non-judgemental if I need to talk really personally.*

> P & J – *both really good at cheering me up and taking my mind off things.*

> Mum – *good for practical advice and a kick up the bum if I need it.*

> Brother – *good for most things though can get angry if I need to talk about ex.*

> C – *good for an intellectual philosophical chat that usually warms my soul.*

If you use email, remember that some people may be available for you to talk to even if they can't reply straight away. A one-way conversation may not be ideal, but if you're feeling particularly alone or there's something you want to get off your chest, you can email or write to a friend at any time you like. You may not get a response for a few days, but at least it's one that you can always keep. Using the internet for one-to-one instant chat on MSN or similar can be another excellent way of keeping in touch with friends who can't talk easily on the phone or meet in person. The phone requires our full attention, and meeting up means one of you has to leave the house, which may be difficult if you have children or there are geographic limitations. Instant chat can give you and friends the opportunity to chat on and off all evening while continuing with other commitments.

Many people worry about being a burden on their friends, especially when they're going through a difficult time, but this is very rarely the case. Most friends want to be available as much as they possibly can, but many aren't able to give as much time as they'd like without their own relationships or other areas of their lives suffering. Having a number of friends you can keep in touch with in a number of ways, and knowing what kind of friend you really need at what time, can help you to spread your friendship needs. That's not to say that if you're lucky enough to have a best friend who is available and able to meet most of your needs that you shouldn't just contact that person. If that's not your situation, however, then you can feel more confident knowing that you have a choice of people to contact.

DEEPENING FRIENDSHIPS

Looking back at your needs list in your notebook, you will almost certainly have found that there were some needs that were not being met by anybody around you. Perhaps these were roles your ex played, or it may be that no one has ever met those needs for you.

The increased solitude of divorce provides an excellent opportunity to reappraise your emotional and psychological needs and to turn to friends to provide you with a deeper level of support than you may have previously received. In turn, it is a chance for you to think about how deepening your relationships with others may provide them with more of what they need.

Many relationships will deepen automatically during a time of crisis for either person. The perfunctory 'how are you?' with the standard reply is usually replaced with more openness about painful and difficult feelings. Some relationships may need a bit of a push, though. How long you've been friends with someone, and your individual experiences of intimacy in other relationships, will impact how easy it is for you to get closer. Intimacy is based on how well you know someone, on how much of your lives and yourselves you share with each other. When we talk about the difficult stuff and feel understood and accepted, our trust grows further and we begin to feel even closer. It's a positive upward spiral.

The early stages of deepening a relationship require risk, however. It means moving beyond the clichéd 'Yes, I'm fine, how are you?' responses and saying how you really feel. A friend who is open and receptive to going deeper will listen respectfully without judging, and offer words of comfort, support and understanding. If you do not get the response you hoped for, this could mean that they don't want to have a deeper relationship than you already have, or it could simply mean that your unusual candour has caught them off guard. Just in case it's the latter, do try to deepen the quality of your conversations on at least two or three occasions before giving up.

When you do begin to open up more about your deeper feelings, you'll soon begin to find that your friends will open up more to you about theirs. This not only helps you feel less isolated with your problems, but also allows you to begin to address some of your unmet needs. When Yolanda began to talk to friends about not feeling acknowledged, included, reassured and valued, she automatically got her other two unmet needs met – being heard and understood. Her friends were able to explore with her how they could help her get more of her needs met.

EXPANDING FRIENDSHIPS

Making new friends is difficult – especially if you need them. It's one thing to be friendly and chatty in a social environment when it doesn't really matter if the person you're talking to likes you or not or ever wants to see you again; but if you feel that you really *need* new friends, then the risk of rejection is greater because you have more to lose.

The first challenge is deciding who you want to be friends with. Are you looking for a friend who you can go down the pub with or to the gym? Someone you can talk to about the children? Someone who's been through a divorce themselves who you can share your experiences with? The kind of friendship you're looking for will narrow down the people with whom you may risk an approach.

The first place to look is within the casual acquaintances you already have and the social groups you're a part of. There's a good chance that your new drinking buddy, gym mate, parenting confidante or even best friend is actually someone you already know. Before you start interviewing strangers at bus stops, think about all the people around you: people at work, in your community, at the places where you regularly go such as the gym or school, and friends of friends. What do you already know about these people? What do you already have in common with them?

If nobody is coming to mind, then you'll need to go back a step and get yourself involved in more social groups. That could mean joining a local community group or committee; starting a new activity, hobby or evening class; or becoming a regular visitor to your pub, art gallery, swimming pool or church. Whatever you choose, make sure it's something you have a genuine interest in. There is no point joining a stamp collecting club where you'll be surrounded by stamp enthusiasts if you have no interest whatsoever in the subject. If, however, you join or visit something that you enjoy, then not only will you automatically have something in common, but you've already got a starting point for conversations too.

Making the first move to develop a friendship is a risk, but remember that this is very much a mutual engagement. At the outset, as well as finding out if someone has an interest in being friends with you, you're also finding out if they are the sort of person you want to be friends with. An initial conversation (especially if you've never spoken before) is likely to be about something fairly general and easy. The great British example is the weather. If you want to be a bit more original then think about a topic that you would expect both of you to be interested in. If you're at the gym then you might talk about sports or fitness; if it's at the school gate then about a forthcoming or recent school event. It doesn't really matter what it is as long as there's a better than average chance they'll have something to say on the matter.

When you start a conversation, try to keep it as open as possible. Saying something like 'The weather's nice today' or 'Liverpool played well' or 'Did you see the school play?' may elicit only a one-word response. Ideally, what you want is to open a conversation and find out a bit more about them. So it would be better to say something like 'How are you enjoying the weather at the moment?' or 'How did you think Liverpool played?' or 'What did you think of the school play?' This is much more likely not only to start a conversation but also to give you an opportunity to evaluate their response. As the conversation develops, you can make a decision about whether or not you want to take it further. That might simply mean that you continue the conversation, or that you make a decision to seek out and chat to that person on a regular basis. If conversation continues to flow well, then the next step would be to make it more personal, such as an invitation for coffee or a drink, or to share a lift or go to an event together. Again, don't let yourself be put off immediately if the answer is no. They may have a very practical reason for not being able to accept on this occasion, but next time may be more convenient.

It takes time, commitment and energy for any friendship to develop. If you continue to like the person you're speaking to, and you're genuinely interested in finding out more about them and letting them know more about you, it's well worth the time and effort.

Deal Effectively with Money and Other Practical Matters

Divorce and separation inevitably bring a whole host of practical and economic changes. Some of those changes may be positive, but many may be a struggle, especially in the early days. This step will begin by helping you to identify the economic and practical resources you already have to hand. Then we'll look at the challenges that you may be facing, including living on a budget and living alone. Finally, we'll work through some strategies and techniques for overcoming some of these difficulties, as well as looking at the divorce process itself.

CHAPTER 13

Identifying Your Economic and
Practical Resources

Becoming single can have significant financial and practical implications for many people. You will almost certainly have less income, your expenditure may increase and you'll be left to run a home on your own. Children will continue to be a joint responsibility, but on a day-to-day basis or when you have contact, you'll be left to manage alone.

For some, how they'll cope on a practical level is the most worrying aspect of a divorce, particularly if they've always relied heavily on a partner or if they feel there are limited resources. This is where doing an economic and practical resource inventory helps. Some things may be difficult, and others perhaps downright impossible, but in this section we're going to focus on all the things you *have* and the things you *can* do.

FINANCE

If you've always been the one who did the finances in your household, then you may already have a good grip on how things are going to pan out. Or, if this is very new to you, you may be wondering where on earth to start. But you really don't need a maths degree to feel in control of your finances. You just need to dig out the relevant figures and get a pen and a calculator.

If you've already drawn up a financial settlement with your ex then you'll probably know most of the final figures. If you haven't, then you can work with estimates to start off with and then firm them up later. Indeed, completing the following exercise will put you in a stronger position to negotiate a financial settlement when you're ready to do so.

YOUR ASSETS AND DEBTS

Start by listing all your individual assets. If you don't yet have a finalised financial settlement, include your joint assets too. This list will include things like your home; any valuable possessions such as art, antiques, collectibles or jewellery; your car; other properties, savings, stocks and shares. List any liquid assets too – those that you can't spend now but will be worth something in the future – such as pension schemes, life insurance, health insurance, savings plans or ISAs and trust funds.

Now list your debts, again looking at individual and joint debts. Remember things like credit cards, store cards, car or other loans and the mortgage. Use actual figures wherever possible and put an 'e' next to any figures that are estimates. Once you've completed this you can add all your assets together and deduct your debts to give you your equity.

This equity figure is used by many solicitors to help negotiate a fair financial split. Nowadays, most solicitors will try to encourage what's known as a clean break settlement. That means that the equity is split in such a way that the payment is final and there is no comeback for either party. An additional payment, often referred to as maintenance, may be made if one person's salary significantly outweighs the other and there isn't enough equity to redress the balance. If there are children, then child support will be paid until the child leaves full-time education. If your final figure was a minus number

ASSETS	House	£	
	Car	£	
	Valuables	£	
	Savings	£	
	Other	£	
LIQUID ASSETS	Pension	£	
	Savings plan	£	
	Life insurance	£	
	ISAs	£	
	Other	£	
	TOTAL	£	
DEBTS	Credit cards	£	
	Car loan	£	
	Mortgage	£	
	Other	£	
	TOTAL		
		EQUITY (assets – debts)	

then this is known as negative equity and a solicitor can advise on how this can be divided.

If you have a lot of equity tied up in your home then selling it and buying two smaller properties may be the best solution. For many people, home is a very important place and it can be heartbreaking to think of having to move from it, especially if it also means moving children. Thinking of your house as an asset rather than a home can help to separate your emotions from what may have to be a purely pragmatic decision.

CASH FLOW

Once you've calculated your equity, it's time to look at your cash flow. You can do this by listing your income and your expenditure in an average month. Remember to include wages, benefits, rental income and any interest from savings in your income column. A template is provided below which lists many common expenses, but is by no means exhaustive, and you may need to add others of your own.

Income	Wages Benefits Other Child support (if agreed) Maintenance (if agreed)	
	TOTAL £	
Expenditure	Mortgage/Rent Electricity/Gas Council tax Water rates Insurance (property/health/life/pet) Television/Phone/Mobiles Car (petrol, tax, insurance) Food Clothing Kids' sundries (pocket money, dinner money, out-of-school lessons) Membership fees Other Child support (if agreed) Maintenance (if agreed)	
	TOTAL: £	
	BALANCE REMAINING: £	

Deducting your expenditure from your income will give you your monthly balance remaining. Remember there will be occasional extras like the boiler breaking down or car maintenance or even a well-earned holiday, so it's always worth having a bit of excess in savings.

OTHER RESOURCES

Before we finalise this financial inventory, it may be worth exploring if you have any other financial resources or opportunities. Perhaps you have a particular skill that you could turn into potential income. Could you get favourable rates on loans through work or a family scheme, or perhaps you have wealthy friends or family who want to help you out? You may feel very strongly about not borrowing from friends; if so, then it would be wrong for you to do so, but it's worth considering if you could accept a gift or some sort of investment, bearing in mind the tax implications. As adults, it's often difficult to accept financial help, but remember that friends and family are there to support you in any way they can. Ask yourself honestly if you would do the same for them if your positions were reversed. If you would, then shouldn't you find the grace to accept their offer, knowing that one day, if you can, you'll do the same?

Having completed these exercises you may have found out that you're better off than you thought, or you may have discovered that you're worse off. If it's the latter, then please don't despair. It may not feel like it right now, but it really is much better to have a realistic knowledge of your financial situation, whether it's good or bad. If you now know that you have less equity than you thought and that your expenditure outstrips your income, at least you can begin to work out how to overcome it (for more on this, see Chapter 15).

PRACTICAL RESOURCES

There are some people who relish the chance to be totally self-sufficient after a divorce. They can be master of their own destiny, eat when they like and what they like, do DIY when and if they like, live like a slob or finally have the home kept clean and tidy. For many, though, self-sufficiency is a heavy burden – especially if it includes parenting.

If you've always been a bit of a perfectionist or a worrier, then it may be particularly difficult to adapt to a single life. A lack of time or money may mean that there are some things that you simply can't do any more, and others that only get half done or done badly. With a bit of brainstorming, however, we often find that there are more resources around us than we think.

THE TASKS YOU NEED TO DO

Let's start by doing a practical inventory of all the tasks that need to be done in an average week. You can use the checklist below as a prompt, ticking the activities that relate to you and adding any additional ones that you think of.

Work: Full-time
Part-time
Voluntary commitments

Personal: Getting exercise
Relaxation time
Evening classes

Home: Cooking
Cleaning
Laundry
Shopping
Gardening

Children: Childcare
Chauffeuring
Entertaining
Organising activities
Homework

Occasional Extras: Car maintenance
Decorating
DIY
Plumbing/Electrics
IT maintenance

Other:

Go through the checklist and cross off any items that you could stop doing altogether, either temporarily until life is a bit more settled, or permanently. You may have been looking for an excuse to get off the PTA for years! You might decide that your children are actually old enough to walk to school alone or catch a bus, and that you'll postpone your Spanish evening class till another time.

Now you need to break down your list into three columns. The first one is a list of the things you can easily achieve; the second is the things you can ask for help with; and the third is the things you could pay someone else to do.

Before you do this, you need to brainstorm friends and family members who could provide you with practical help. These may not necessarily be people you would ask on a regular basis, but they may be people who could help in a crisis. For instance, you may know a number of people who would baby-sit on an occasional evening, and a friend of a friend who's a computer whiz who you could call if your system crashes. You might also remember that your dad's been offering to take over the garden for years.

Some people find it difficult to ask others to do something for them. If you've always been independent, then you may feel like it's some sort of admission of failure or weakness to ask for practical support. In actual fact, however, when we ask friends and family for favours, we're often doing them a favour as well. Most people like to help. They want to feel useful and needed. When we open up to others and ask, we're fulfilling those needs for them; and we're also making it easier for them to ask us for favours in return. Relationships are about giving and receiving – and right now it's your time to receive.

This is what your final list might look like:

CAN DO	FRIENDS/FAMILY	PAY SOMEONE
Work	Jill's hubby is IT expert	Ironing
Cooking	Dad take kids to dance	Online food shop
Cleaning	June baby-sit occasionally	

This may still leave you with quite a list of things you know you're going to struggle with, and we'll begin to look at how you can overcome these in Chapter 15. Hopefully, though, you've found at least a few things that you can worry about less.

CHAPTER 14

Recognising Financial and Practical Challenges

Living alone, with or without children, is a challenge for many newly separated couples. Undoubtedly there are a few who find life much easier without someone else to look after, but for most, there are a myriad of practical difficulties to be overcome. In this section we're going to explore what some of those difficulties may be. Some of them may not affect you at the moment, but thinking ahead about the challenges you may face in the future can help you to be better prepared.

MONEY

Divorce can have massive financial implications for many people, so unless you've got lots of excess cash, you're going to feel the pinch. Your first challenge will be deciding whether or not one of you can afford to stay in the original home, and if so, what financial cutbacks you might need to make to allow this. If you can't afford it, then you may be looking to buy a smaller property or one in a cheaper area, or to rent somewhere. Whatever you do, there will be costs at a financial and practical level.

You'll need to think about where you'll make financial cutbacks. Will this affect your children's life, and yours? Will you need to cut down on social activities, heating and phone bills, car running costs? Will you have to do without those added extras like special food items, bottles of wine, nice toiletries or rented DVDs and takeaways? How long do you expect these cutbacks to last? Weeks? Months? Years?

Financial sacrifices may seem just like an irritation at first, but if they continue for a long time then feelings of resentment can build. This is particularly so if the cutbacks affect your children, such as no longer being able to afford piano lessons, trendy trainers or the annual school trip; or when you see friends who can easily afford the latest flat-screen television, theatre tickets or round of drinks in the pub.

You may not have been used to living on a budget in the past, or perhaps your partner managed financial things. Now it will be up to you to pay bills and balance the books every month, and make sure you keep enough by for when the car tax runs out. Managing finances, however meagre they may be, comes naturally to some people, but for others it's a headache.

HOUSING

If you're moving house, what difference will your new location make? Will you be further from shops, work or school? Will you need to make more time for travelling? How might it affect your children and your ability to keep in touch with family and friends?

SPLITTING POSSESSIONS

Another issue that affects pretty much everyone is splitting possessions. In Chapter 8 we looked at some of the emotional implications of losing familiar things around you, but there are also practical ones. What items will you learn to live without – for example, a dishwasher, yoghurt maker or DVD recorder? What things do you need to replace urgently, and what can you replace over time? For example, you might take your time to replace a mirror for the hallway, a digital camera or an electric drill, but you should urgently consider getting things like jump leads for the car, a set of screwdrivers, a tin opener and a torch. These are the kinds of items that you may not use every day, but when you need them, you need them urgently. If this has triggered some thoughts in your mind then write them on a shopping list NOW!

DEALING WITH EMERGENCIES

You need to be able to deal with emergencies on your own. Do you know where the stop cock is, when you might need it and what to do with it if you do? Do you have a trip switch or a circuit breaker? Where would you switch off the electricity or the gas if you needed to? If you've moved location, you might also want to find out the number of a local plumber, electrician and taxi firm, and check where the nearest A&E is. Hopefully, you won't ever need any of this information, but some things are better not left to luck.

STORAGE

Another issue that might arise is the need to put things in storage. If you're moving into a smaller place or into furnished rented accommodation then you may find that there are some things that just won't fit anywhere. You'll need to make a decision about whether to chuck or store them. If you're lucky, your friends may be able to accommodate a few boxes for you or find a place for Grandma's rocking chair, otherwise you'll need to check the price of storage.

DAY-TO-DAY LIVING

There are many things to work out when you first start living alone. Although it can feel quite liberating for some people, niggling practical issues can crop up. Most couples manage to share at least some of the tasks around the home, but when you're alone, it will all fall to you. You may be confident that you can manage most tasks, but now may be the time to think about where your skills could be polished up.

Below is a list of common tasks, in no particular order. Take a few moments to run through the list and mark them with either a tick to indicate okay, a cross if it's a problem and a question mark if you're not sure.

House cleaning
Laundry
Ironing
Shopping
Cooking
Driving
Gardening
Car cleaning
Car maintenance
Paying bills
Managing finances
Looking after pets
Looking after plants
Setting up the DVD
Computer maintenance
Using the boiler/central heating timer
Changing light bulbs
General DIY
Lifts for kids
Entertainment for kids
Homework with kids

If there are any extra things that have come to mind while reading through this, add them to the list and mark them with a tick, cross or question mark as appropriate.

On top of the day-to-day responsibilities of running the home and looking after children, you may also want to keep up or begin relaxation or social activities. Have a think about how feasible this is going to be and whether or not you will still have the time, the money or the baby-sitting resources. If some activities will be difficult, consider different options, such as doing a workout to a DVD at home if you can't get a baby-sitter, or postponing the Spanish lessons till next term.

KEEPING UP THE DAY JOB

If you're working full-time or part-time and you need the income then you probably won't have the option to stop. However, you may want to consider taking some holiday time for yourself to reflect on your changing situation. If that isn't possible, then you need to consider whether you'd benefit from making any changes to your work to enable you to cope or function well during this time of change. For example, many people prefer not to take up a promotion or extra responsibilities while they're going through a divorce. Or you could think about whether there are any duties that you could cut back on, just for a short while, until you're back on your feet again. Many employers are sympathetic to the stress that divorce can create and will do what they can to help you through this difficult time, rather than risk losing you.

If you're a full-time parent, you may do voluntary or committee work as well. If this is the case, then you'll need to work out if you can continue with these commitments – not just from the practical point of view of being there but also in terms of whether or not you'll have the emotional and psychological energy. For some people, continuing with external activities is essential for their sense of wellbeing, but others decide to take a break, at least for a while, until life has settled.

Keeping life going as normally as possible, while making allowances for the fact that divorce is bound to be a struggle, is always a difficult balance. Therefore we need to cut ourselves some slack where we can. Only you can make the decision about what you can cope with at the moment, but remember that it is okay to slow down for a while.

CHAPTER 15

Your Action Plan

Becoming single again faces us with many challenges, both practical and emotional. At a time when you may be struggling to motivate yourself enough to get out of bed in the morning, you've also got to continue to hold down a job and look after your home and children. It's a tough time, but one that can make you realise you're much stronger and more resourceful than you thought.

In Chapter 13 we explored your economic and practical resources. Working through the exercises in that chapter will have given you an overview of your current financial situation and a practical inventory of the tasks that need to be done over an average week. In Chapter 14 you may have highlighted some areas where you already struggle or suspect that you might in the future. This may have included financial aspects as well as issues related to the day-to-day challenge of living alone. Now we're going to focus on how you move forward in these essential areas.

TAKING CONTROL OF YOUR FINANCES

There are many different ways of managing your finances, and which you choose will depend on your previous experience and personal preference. First, you need to set up a basic bank account in your name, if you haven't already done so. You'll need at least a current account for paying income into and paying bills, and a savings account for putting a bit of money aside (however small). You might find it useful to have two savings accounts: one for short-term savings (perhaps for extra purchases or holidays) and a long-term savings account for rainy day items and larger investments such as a new car or long-haul holiday. Different building societies and banks offer various products with different interest rates and incentives, so do shop around before you make your final decision. Look out for any tax-free entitlements, such as cash ISAs.

Once your bank accounts are set up, you'll need to think about how you'll keep a record of your income and expenditure. For some people a basic pen and paper system works best, entering figures on a daily or weekly basis. Most stationers sell cash books that have columns pre-printed for income, expenditure and balance. If you don't want to use pen and paper then you could create a template on a computer spreadsheet programme such as Excel and let the computer do the maths for you. This has the advantage that you can cut and paste regular items such as standing orders and direct debits rather than having to rewrite them each month. Or you may decide to buy a proprietary software package to manage your finances, such as Microsoft Money. These packages allow you to analyse your spending in different areas, such as food, clothing or motor expenses, and to do a forecast with a single press of a button.

Whatever system you choose, you still have to do the donkey work of entering your figures on a regular basis. This can seem tedious at times, but it really is the only way to keep track of where your money goes.

LEARNING TO BUDGET

Most people are worse off financially after a separation. Consequently, budgeting may need to become a way of life, at least for a while. Looking back at the cash flow you created in

Chapter 13, you now need to seriously consider the areas of spending where you can cut back. Can you become more economical with gas, electricity or phone use to reduce your utility bills? Can you reduce your food bill by buying more home brands or fewer pre-prepared products? Can you give up a bottle of wine, make packed lunches for the kids or cut down on petrol costs by using the car less? You'll need to get creative to think about areas where you can economise. If you're struggling for ideas then talk to friends, preferably poorer ones. Ask them if they have any tips on cutting back, and find out what their average spend is on different things. There are also some great books on living on a budget which will give you some ideas. Some cutbacks will be more painful than others. You may need to consider going out less or cancelling your membership at the gym, or trading your car for a cheaper and more economical model.

You may be able to reduce your expenditure further by switching your mortgage to someone with a lower interest rate. Check whether you're eligible for discounts on council tax or water rates. You may also be entitled to other benefits, or you might think about increasing your income by taking an extra job or renting out a room in your home.

If, after making all the cutbacks you possibly can and maximising your income, you still have a regular shortfall, then talk to one of the national financial advisory services listed in the Further Help section at the end of this book (see page 203).

Living with limited income can become depressing, but remember that this is usually a short-term problem. As you earn more or the children become less dependent, your standard of living should improve. In the meantime, living contentedly on a shoestring is all about attitude. Focusing on what you *don't* have will undoubtedly make you miserable, whereas making yourself appreciate the things you do have can make you feel like the richest person on earth. A period of poverty can help us to focus on taking pleasure in the simple things of life: a walk in the park, a bowl of homemade soup, and spending time with the people we love.

FINANCIAL AGREEMENTS, CHILD SUPPORT AND MAINTENANCE

The other avenue of your finances that you need to explore thoroughly is the agreement you've made with your ex. If you don't have a formal agreement in place and you're struggling financially, then it's definitely worth making an appointment to see a solicitor and finding out your legal entitlements. If you have children, then it's even more important that arrangements have been formalised in order to protect their current and future welfare.

When choosing a solicitor, make sure it's someone you feel you can talk to, someone who listens to you and understands where you're coming from. You need to be confident that they'll provide reliable advice and that they'll let you make your own decisions. They should also help you understand the consequences of the decisions that you make. A good solicitor will be able to look at your individual circumstances and advise you on the options available to you while ensuring that the welfare of the children comes first. Resolution is an organisation that specialises in family law. All their members aim to help separating couples achieve a constructive settlement of their differences in a way that avoids protracted arguments and promotes co-operation between parents in decisions concerning children. (For details, see Further Help, page 203.)

Many solicitors offer a free first appointment. This can be really useful for establishing whether or not you think you can work with them on an ongoing basis. They will also tell you whether or not you're eligible for help with legal fees through the Community Legal Service (Legal Aid). You might find it helpful to make a list of questions you want to ask and take notes while you're there so you don't forgot anything important.

If you already have a financial agreement but either your or your ex's circumstances have changed, then it may be worth going back to your solicitor to find out if any adjustments in maintenance or child support are possible. The CSA (Child Support Agency) is still involved in many disputes about payments, but the system is currently under review so do check with your solicitor or with your local Citizens Advice Bureau before contacting them.

THE DIVORCE PROCEDURE

Some people want to get the legal procedure of divorce underway as soon as possible while others see this purely as a formality that can wait for many years after the relationship has ended. There is no right and wrong. One thing that is worth considering, though, is the cost of divorce. If there is still a lot of acrimony between you and your ex, then a divorce is more likely to be long and drawn out and therefore expensive. Waiting until emotions have calmed down may make the legal process smoother and cheaper for everyone involved.

When you're ready to proceed, you can either go through a solicitor or you can do it yourself by buying a divorce kit or using one of the many online services. Either way, the procedure is basically like this. It begins with a petition and ends with a decree absolute, which dissolves the marriage. The timescale to complete the process differs from case to case, but even the most straightforward cases take four to six months. If you have children, then part of the divorce process will include a Statement of Arrangements for children. This document shows that all the necessary arrangements to look after and financially support the children have been made. Since this is needed before the divorce can be finalised, it's best to have agreed all these details with your ex either alone, through mediation or via solicitors before you begin divorce proceedings.

There is only one 'ground' for divorce, and that is that the marriage has irretrievably broken down. This is proved by establishing the existence of one of five factual circumstances. These are:

➤ Your spouse has committed adultery and you find it intolerable to continue to live with him/her.

➤ Your spouse has behaved in such a way that it would be unreasonable to expect you to continue to live with him/her.

➤ Your spouse has deserted you for a continuous period of two years or more.

➤ You have been living apart from your spouse for two years or more and your spouse agrees to the divorce.

➤ You have been living apart from your spouse for five years or more, whether or not your spouse agrees to the divorce.

It is no longer compulsory in a petition based on adultery to name the third person concerned.

The divorce process will be much simpler if both of you have agreed the reasons for the divorce. If a divorce is contested then the procedure can take much longer. In a nutshell, the process is as follows:

The person who starts the divorce, known as the 'Petitioner', sends a divorce petition to the court, along with a Statement of Arrangements for children, marriage certificate and a court fee. A copy of these is then sent to your partner, known as the 'Respondent', together with a form of acknowledgement to complete and return within eight days. Assuming the Respondent does not disagree and decide to defend the petition, the Petitioner's solicitor prepares an Affidavit (a sworn statement) which confirms that the contents of the petition are true. This is then sent to the court with a request for a date for pronouncement of the provisional decree of divorce, known as the 'Decree Nisi'. A judge then looks through the papers, decides if the Petitioner is entitled to a divorce, checks that the Statement of Arrangements for Children is sufficient and mutually agreed, and certifies that Decree Nisi can be pronounced. The Petitioner and Respondent will be notified of the date of the hearing but are not required to attend. If the judge is unhappy with the arrangements for children they may request further information or ask the Petitioner and Respondent to attend an informal appointment to clarify and explore areas of concern. A copy of the Decree Nisi will be sent to both the Petitioner and the Respondent, and once a minimum of six weeks and one day has passed, the Petitioner may apply for Decree Absolute. Once this is received the marriage is legally dissolved.

If the divorce is defended then the Respondent must file a defence, known as an 'Answer', and the respective solicitors will attempt to find acceptable mutual ground before reapplying to court. If there is no agreement, for example where one party does not wish to be divorced, then ultimately a court will determine whether there should be a divorce. Be warned, however: defended divorces are held in open court and can be attended by the public and/or press. Subjecting yourself, and your family, to this kind of exposure should not be a decision that's taken lightly.

LIVING OR PARENTING ALONE

Whether you're divorced or not, financially stretched or well off, you still have to cope with the day-to-day pressures of living alone. If you have kids, you also have to deal with lone parenting. In Chapter 13 you created a list of all the tasks and activities you have to achieve in an average week, and you considered whether or not you could delegate any of them to anyone else. In Chapter 14 you considered if there were any things you would struggle with. If there were, now is the time to make some SPORT goals (see page 92). So if you realised that you know nothing about DIY or that you really need to learn how to cook, write it as a SPORT goal. Remember to say how you'll achieve your goal (reading a book, asking a friend, going on a course) and also specify a date by which you want to achieve your goal.

With your skills now taken care of, it's time to look at whether your week can run more smoothly. One of the simplest ways to do this is to create a weekly schedule for yourself. Start by drawing a simple table with the days of the week and times of day on it, and put down everything that's unchangeable, such as work and commitments to children. Then put down the things you really want to be able to continue to do. That might be seeing friends, maintaining an exercise routine or a hobby, or just watching a favourite television programme.

Now you need to get another sheet of paper and list all the other routine and occasional activities that you want to put into your schedule. Make a note, too, of roughly how much time each thing takes. Your final task is to try and fit these things into your schedule. How much you cram into each day is very much a matter of choice. Some people would prefer to be very, very busy on one day and then take it easier the next. Some people like to do a bit of housework each day or buy food for tea each day, while others prefer to work like stink and get everything out of the way at once. It really doesn't matter how you do it, as long as it works for you and your family.

However you plan your schedule, make sure you have some 'free' time. There will undoubtedly be things you've forgotten or occasional things you need to do which you can slot into that time. More importantly, though, you need time just for yourself to unwind and relax.

Below is an example of how one mother of a nine-year-old boy scheduled her week. She decided that doing Tom's reading and spellings in the morning worked better for both of them, and when he had homework he would do it in the kitchen while she was cooking tea so he could ask any questions he needed to. She also decided that buying something for tea each day when she bought her sandwich for lunch not only meant that they ate fresher food each night, but also gave her more free time at the weekend. Her parents liked it if they visited once a week so she decided to ask if her mum would do tea each week to give her a night off. Her mum was delighted. Tom spent alternate weekends with his dad, so she would try to schedule any major tasks or the occasional weekend away for when he wasn't there.

New schedules take time to get used to and need to be flexible to cope with life's changes. If you have children then your schedule may often need to change to make allowances for their changing needs. Trying to stay as flexible but as organised as possible will help you to keep on top of all the things you need to do. Ultimately, though, do remember that the most important thing you can do is enjoy your life, your family and your friends. For most of us, earning an income is not optional, but doing housework is. Yes, you do have to feed yourself and keep the place hygienic, but if the sheets aren't washed for another week the sky will not collapse on you. Make sure you always make time for the things that matter.

	Monday	Tuesday	Wednesday	Thursday	Friday
7.00	Read to Tom	Read to Tom	Spellings with Tom	Spellings with Tom	Exercise
9.00	Work	Work	Work	Work	Work
1.00	Lunch/food shop	Lunch/food shop	Lunch/food shop	Lunch/food shop	Lunch with friend
2.00	Work	Work	Work	Work	Work
5.30	Cook/ Homework	Cook/ Homework	Tea at Mum and Dad's	Cook/ Homework	Tom football and takeaway
7.30	TV/ironing	Exercise	Free	Free	TV night with Tom

	Saturday (alternate no Tom)	Sunday
AM	Food shop and chores	Free
PM	Alternate weeks: gardening or updating finances	Free
EVE	Go out or television	Get Tom ready to go back to school

Learn to Communicate Effectively with Your Ex

Communication is the key to resolving differences and finding compromises for the future. In the short term at least, both you and your ex will need to communicate in order to sort out the practicalities of your separation. If you share children, it is a skill you'll need to develop for life. Unfortunately, breakdowns in communication are often the cause of divorce so it can be particularly difficult to try and achieve something when you've always failed before. However, this step aims to give you some new techniques to try as well as covering the essential skills you'll need in order to co-parent effectively.

CHAPTER 16

Putting Children First

If you've got children then the bottom line is this: you are responsible for behaving in a way, and making decisions, that will always be in the best interests of your children, *in spite* of what you may be feeling emotionally.

It doesn't matter what your ex has done, or how, or who with. Your children's needs must still come first. That means that unless there are safety concerns or other obvious reasons why your children shouldn't have contact, they need to maintain a healthy relationship with both you and your ex. You can either support and encourage that relationship or, because of your anger, sadness, guilt or indifference, you can make that relationship very uncomfortable indeed. Even if a child is feeling hurt and angry and saying they don't want to see your ex, it's still up to you to create an environment where they can change their mind, otherwise you will increase the risk that they'll lose a parent for ever.

The Relate guide, *Help Your Children Cope with Your Divorce*, gives clear advice and guidance on how to minimise the impact of parental separation. It looks in depth at things such as breaking the news, how children react, managing leaving day, establishing new routines and common parenting problems.

CO-PARENTING COMMUNICATION

First and foremost, always try and separate the discussions you need to have about the children from all other conversations.

Make it clear that your goal is to reach an agreement for the children's benefit. They are your mutual agenda and your mutual goal. By agreeing this up front, hopefully both of you can contain any difficult emotions associated with your separation.

Second, never have these conversations – or any other potentially difficult discussions – in front of the children if you can avoid it. Evidence has shown that it is the conflict and tension between separating parents that damages children, so the easiest way to minimise that is to ensure they aren't around. It also means that they're not tempted to try and chip in and offer help to one side or the other. The conversation is between the two of you and should remain so.

If it's really difficult to have a constructive conversation face to face, then try telephone or email instead. Many couples find this a much simpler and more stress-free way of communicating, and email has the added advantage of providing each of you with a written copy of what's been said. This can be particularly useful for confirming contact details or financial arrangements about the kids.

When you do speak in front of the children, which will happen at handover times or school or family events you both attend, make sure you're calm and courteous. Even if deep down inside you hate each other, for your children's sake show them that you can still both behave like rational human beings and treat each other with basic respect and decency. Make a pact with yourself, too, that you will never put your ex down in front of your children. When you do this, you're not just undermining the other parent, but also part of your children. Since they share the same genes, criticising their parent means criticising them too.

Finally, never use your children as messengers or go-betweens. This puts children in an impossible position where they have to remember a message accurately and try and deliver it in a tone that won't upset the other parent. They then have to cope with the reaction of the other parent and make a decision about what to do with any spoken or unspoken information they receive. Dad, for example, might tut, roll his eyes and sigh a reluctant 'Okay, tell your mum I said yes.' It's all far too big a responsibility for a child of any age, and with texting, email and the phone, there really is no excuse for it nowadays.

BREAKING THE NEWS

The best way to break the news of your separation is together. This shows children that you're united in your decision, and reinforces the message that you're going to be working together to find the best possible solutions for the family. How much you tell them of the actual reasons for your separation will depend on their age and maturity. The general rule should be to ensure that they understand that it is the marriage that has broken down, not the family; and even though you no longer love each other, both of you still love them in exactly the same way as you always have.

Make sure the two of you have discussed and agreed what you're going to say and, if at all possible, tell the children that it's a mutual decision. This will stop them feeling that they should take sides. Give them plenty of reassurance that they're still going to see both of you, and that although life will be very different and tough for a while, it's going to be okay.

Try to brainstorm the questions they may ask and discuss what your answers will be. For example, what will the new living arrangements be; when will changes happen; what will you do about holidays and Christmas; where will the cat go? The more prepared you are for their questions, the more in control you will both feel; consequently, the more secure your children will feel about the future.

MANAGING EVERYONE'S FEELINGS

Separation is one of the most painful and distressing events that anyone will experience, and it will affect everyone in the family. Wherever possible, you and your ex need to make sure that you protect your children from the overwhelming emotions you may sometimes feel. That doesn't mean you have to pretend that everything's okay, but remember that children can be frightened by strong displays of emotion. Sharing that you're sad, worried and angry about what's happening can help them to feel more comfortable expressing their feelings, but make sure you're also giving them plenty of reassurance that you're coping and life is going to be okay.

Children often blame themselves for their parents' divorce, especially if there has been tension in the house that has sometimes come their way. It's important that these feelings are addressed directly and children are told that your decision to separate is not their fault or connected to anything that they've done.

You and your ex should also agree that you will both be available to talk to the children whenever they need to. It's important to maintain an open-door policy to address their concerns and feelings over the coming weeks and months. When your children do talk to you, make sure you include the other parent in any decisions that need to be made. Children need to know that the two of you will be continuing to work together for them, and that you value and respect the other parent as a mum or a dad, even though you'll no longer be a married couple.

ESTABLISHING LIVING AND CONTACT ARRANGEMENTS

When trying to decide what arrangements will work for you, your priority should be thinking about what your children will need. Obviously, you'll need to consider geographic and financial practicalities, but experts agree that it's best to maintain as much of the status quo as you can. That means maximum access to both of you and as few changes to school, friends and other routines as possible.

When one or both of you is hurting or angry, it's tempting to use your children as a weapon against each other. The more committed your ex is as a parent, the more powerful the weapon of limiting contact with their children will be. Remember, though, no matter how badly you may feel you've been treated in your relationship, your ex can still be an excellent parent, and your children need the love and support of both of you.

THE FIRST YEAR

If you've got children, then you and your ex are always going to need to stay in contact. No amount of pre-planning in the world is going to prepare you for the changes that are to come. What's more, kids are wonderfully unpredictable, so any plans you do make can quickly go out of the window and you'll need to rearrange things with your ex. It's essential that the two of you try to remain as flexible as possible to the changes that are to come, many of which will be in the first year.

The first year will contain many firsts for your new-style family. The first Christmas, first birthdays, Mother's/Father's day, first holidays alone, first parents' evenings and sports days. You *and* your ex will need to learn to negotiate about all of these events to find a fair solution that works as well as possible for all of you. You'll also need to manage handover times in a way that shows the children that although you'll miss them, you want them to enjoy seeing their other parent. This is going to be a testing time for both of you as you begin to see each other and relate to each other as co-parents rather than as partners.

NEW PARTNERS

At some time, one or both of you is likely to meet someone else. Indeed, it may be that meeting someone else was the catalyst for ending your marriage. Either way, how you manage this new person in your lives affects not only you, but also your children. If at all possible, it's best not to introduce somebody new until the dust has settled. Children need time to accept the fact that your relationship is over and that you won't be getting back together again. They need to get used to having separate parents in separate homes. When a new person is introduced too soon, children are more likely to feel that a parent is being replaced, even if you've expressly said this isn't the case. Children struggle with split loyalties during even the most amicable divorce, so giving them time to manage these difficult feelings before introducing yet another component is essential.

When your ex introduces their new partner, it's important that you try to support the new union in spite of how you might really be feeling. It's common for old painful feelings to be rekindled but again, for your children's sake, try to remain as neutral as possible so they can make up their own minds. If you're the one who's met someone new, try to curb your enthusiasm and be sensitive to the fact that even though you may think they're great, your kids are going to need some time to get used to this new person and develop their own opinion.

WHEN AN EX WON'T OR CAN'T CO-OPERATE

Unfortunately, not all parents are able to put the needs of their children above their own. That may be because of unresolved anger or guilt, or because of their very real struggle to manage their loss and come to terms with what's happened. In some cases, it may be due to a mental health issue or a substance addiction, or they may be breaking away from a violent or abusive relationship. Every situation is completely different. Your ex may seem determined to thwart your attempts to communicate, no matter how hard you try, but don't give up. See Chapter 17 for more advice on improving your communication skills, but also consider talking to a third party. If your ex has a friend or family member they respect, ask them if they will act as an intermediary. If that doesn't work, you could consider trying a mediation service or, as a last resort, you may need to speak to your solicitor. Whatever course of action you take, remember that your children's needs must come first.

CHAPTER 17

The Art of Effective Communication

Effective communication would be so easy if it involved only one person. Unfortunately, however, it ultimately depends on both you and your partner committing to doing your bit. Even if your ex seems to have absolutely no interest in making your conversations run more smoothly, small changes on your part can make a significant difference to how they respond and how well your conversations flow.

STOPPING NEGATIVE COMMUNICATION PATTERNS

Many couples find that their conversations follow exactly the same predictable patterns. Either they end up arguing, going round and round in circles, or in a stalemate position. If you can change your part of the communication exchange, then you may well be able to steer your conversations onto a new course.

Many couples fall into a very common trap: the parent/child game. There are a few different versions of this game. In one version, one person takes the role of the responsible, sensible parent while the other plays the irresponsible, incompetent child. In another, the critical parent and the naughty child, one person tells off the other and tries to pull them back into line and make them behave properly. The final version is the nurturing, caring parent and the needy child. This time the child is vulnerable and dependent, and the parent is trying to sort everything out for them in an attempt to make them feel better and to stand on their own two feet.

When couples get trapped into games like these, both partners will blame the other for their communication style. The parent will say, 'I wish they'd stop being so childish,' and the child says, 'I wish they'd stop talking to me like I'm a child.' The more the child feels talked down to, patronised, criticised, disrespected and undermined, the more they'll act and talk like a child. They're more likely to get stroppy and sulk, whine and moan or feel incompetent. As the child responds in their childlike way, the parent will become more convinced that they have to try and take control and stay entrenched in their authoritative position. So the cycle continues ad infinitum.

There are other games like the parent/child game. Some couples get stuck in good cop/bad cop, idol/worshipper or fighting like cat and dog. The characters may change but the principle is the same. If you continue to talk like a critical parent, dependent child or bad cop, you will carry on getting the same opposing response. When you change your conver-sation style, your ex will begin to as well. It may take time, but the more you can pull yourself into an equal, adult way of relating, the easier it will be for them to meet you in the same place. To retrain your style, you need to learn how to speak and listen effectively, but first you need to make sure you're fully prepared for the conversation ahead.

BE PREPARED

Your conversations are much more likely to be successful if you know what you want to say and what you want to achieve. In Chapter 9, you may have written some specific goals that you want to reach with your ex, and some of these may have involved talking. If you don't have specific goals already, you can use the SPORT technique (see page 92) to write goals for each conversation you need to have. This can help you to focus on what you want to get out of your conversation and keep you on track.

When considering your goals, you need to decide if you're making a negotiable request, a bottom-line demand or having a discussion. If you're making a request, then you should be clear in your mind about what you want, but you should also think about what you'd be happy to accept. In any relationship, compromise is essential. The reality is that you and your ex won't agree on everything, so before you go into the conversation, make sure you know what your compromise position will be. This will enable you to continue to feel in control while demonstrating generosity and flexibility towards your ex, which hopefully will be reciprocated. If you're going to write down your goals, include your compromise position in them. If the situation you're addressing is non-negotiable, then make that clear for yourself in your goal, and if the conversation is going to be a discussion, then write a goal that expresses the outcome you want to achieve. Here are some examples:

➤ I want to ask my ex to pay 80 per cent towards Tom's school holiday but I would accept 60 per cent.

➤ I want to have the children an extra evening per week starting after Easter, or at least have them for tea one evening. If the latter, then I'd like to re-negotiate in September.

➤ I want my ex to return all keys to the house and to phone before he turns up. This is non-negotiable.

➤ I want to discuss what to do about selling the house and end the conversation with a list of options for us to consider.

➤ I want to talk about the kids' schooling and find out my ex's opinions on what she thinks would be best for their future.

Another essential component of being prepared is thinking about how your ex might respond and how you'll handle their response. If you think they'll get upset or angry or become argumentative, what will you do? The more prepared you are for a negative response, the easier it will be for you to maintain your composure and your objective. You may find rehearsing the conversation with a friend who takes on the role of your argumentative or silent ex a useful way of practising new skills beforehand.

The final part of your preparation is to think about the time and the place for your conversation. Ideally, you should choose neutral territory such as a pub, café or park, and a time when you won't be disturbed and both of you are as stress-free as possible. That means not doing it straight after a busy shift at work or before an important meeting – and turning your mobiles off. You should also make sure that your ex knows that you want to talk and, preferably, what you want to talk about. If you surprise your ex with an important conversation when it's inconvenient to them and they're already stressed out about something else, they're likely to feel ambushed and go straight on the defence. Being prepared is not only good for you; it will also be good for them. If appropriate, you could email your ex to arrange a mutually convenient time and place, and also tell them what you'd like to discuss. This will give them time to think about their response and manage any immediate emotions that might arise. With the necessary emotional and practical preparations done, you should both be ready to talk.

HOW TO SPEAK SO YOUR EX WILL LISTEN

So you've got your time, you've got your place and you've got your agenda. You know what you want to achieve and what compromise you're willing to accept. Now it's down to you to express yourself clearly and honestly, and create an environment where your partner is more likely to listen and respond non-defensively and non-judgementally.

Ideally, your conversation should be as equals, adult to adult. That means you need to make sure you're not talking like a critical parent: 'You should do this, you shouldn't do that'; 'If you don't do ... I'll...' Equally, you need to avoid being the nurturing parent: 'I know this is difficult for you, darling, but...'; or the child: 'If you don't do what I say I'll scream, sulk...' Think about how you talk to friends and how you talk to colleagues at work. Your conversations with your ex should follow the same sort of style. If you find yourself using words or a tone of voice you'd never dream of using at work, then you're slipping out of adult.

In order to convey your message, you need to choose your words carefully. Think about what you're saying and how it may be heard. If you think you're being vague or may be misunderstood, stop and ask and clarify if necessary. Effective communication is about accuracy, not speed. Many of us try to rush difficult conversations to try and get them over and done with. Unfortunately, this often results in misunderstandings which then take even longer to resolve. So if you need to use three words to explain something clearly, do so. That doesn't mean it's okay to waffle on endlessly, but if it's essential that your ex understands a particular point, take the necessary time to explain it.

The most important thing to remember is to stick to your goal. Don't let yourself get sidetracked by your emotions. If you're feeling angry, confused, hurt or disappointed then it may be perfectly appropriate to share that, but don't let that emotion take over and control the conversation. If the goal of your discussion was purely to share how you feel, then ranting, raging, crying and talking about the past may be fine, but if it wasn't then guard your heart and your tongue. If your goal included getting a positive or affirmative response from your ex, then anything provocative from you is much more likely to put them on the defensive and reduce your chance of success. Stay focused on the current moment and what you want for the future, and keep your emotional thoughts and feelings to share with caring friends. Your relationship is over and nothing can change the past. This is about you, now, moving forward – not you two, back then. You can use the following points as a checklist to ensure you are speaking effectively:

➤ No blaming – it doesn't matter whose fault something is; your priority should be moving forward.

➤ No name-calling – any kind of name-calling, however justified you might feel it is, will just cause provocation and take you further from your goals.

➤ No mind reading – even if you had been with your ex for 50 years, you still wouldn't know exactly what's inside their head, so don't risk insult by assuming you know what they think or feel.

➤ Don't drag up the past – no matter how much pain you may still be holding, stick to today and the future, not yesterday.

➤ Don't bring in other people's opinions – let your argument stand on its own merits rather than bringing in other people's views, which may be antagonistic.

➤ Be assertive, not aggressive – (see page 55).

➤ No threats, intimidation, manipulation, whining, moaning or any other form of emotional blackmail.

➤ Stay focused – try not to get distracted by other issues or small talk. You can have those conversations another day, but for now, stick to your goal.

➤ No 'shoulds' or 'shouldn'ts' – it doesn't work in adult conversation.

Ultimately, it doesn't really matter what you say; what matters is what your ex hears. No matter how carefully you choose your words, they may still take offence or challenge you. If that happens, whatever you do, don't get nit-picky or defensive yourself. Remember your goal, apologise, explain what you meant and try to get back on track as quickly as possible.

Try not to expect immediate results. If your ex needs time to think about what you've said, or if their initial response is negative, hold your position and call time. If you've stated your case and your request and there's nothing else for you to say, and your ex isn't asking you for any further information, then leave it at that for the day and reschedule another time to speak. Pushing your ex into a decision they're not ready to make can all too easily backfire. So be patient.

HOW TO LISTEN SO YOUR EX FEELS HEARD

Speaking is only half the story. When you've initiated a conversation then you need to make sure you give your ex plenty of opportunity to respond. There will be occasions when your ex is the one who has approached you with a request or has needed to talk. When this is the case you need to make listening attentively your goal. Whenever your ex is speaking, you need to make sure you're hearing what's being said and that your ex *feels* heard.

The first rule of listening is to listen – not to wait. If we're honest, a lot of the time when we think we're listening, we're actually just waiting for our turn to talk again. When you listen, listen with all of yourself. Make yourself hear each and every word that's spoken. Imagine yourself lost in the middle of nowhere, late for an important appointment and low on petrol. You stop someone and ask for directions. The way you listen to that welcome stranger on the road is the way you should listen to your ex. Give them 100 per cent of your attention and make sure you fully understand what they're saying. Below are some more things to remember when listening:

➤ Don't interrupt – it's just plain rude and annoying.

➤ Ask for clarification – this is the only exception for interrupting. If you really don't understand what's being said, stop and ask for clarification.

➤ Express understanding – make sure you nod and express your understanding by saying 'okay', 'right', 'I understand'.

➤ Express empathy – if you really know what your ex is saying because you've experienced it yourself or you can imagine how it would feel, say so.

➤ Be aware of your body language – give 100 per cent physical attention. Maintain eye contact and don't fidget, yawn, sigh or roll your eyes.

➤ Acknowledge emotions – if your ex expresses a specific emotion then make sure they know you've heard it by repeating it back. For instance, 'I understand that you're angry' or 'I can see that you're upset'.

➤ Repeat essential words and phrases – if something important has been said which you're meant to remember then repeat it back. For example, 'You can't have the children on Tuesday any more' or 'Your job position has become insecure'.

➤ Focus on content, not delivery – if your ex has always irritated you by the way they speak, make sure you keep your focus on the content of what they're saying, not on the way they're saying it. We can't all be perfect orators.

➤ Remain objective – try to keep your emotions in check so that you can stay focused on your goal.

As well as listening to what's being said, try to be aware of any unspoken information you may be picking up. Are they angry, upset, anxious or confused? If so, how might this be influencing what they're saying? If you're picking up on something and you think it's relevant, then check it out. Don't pretend to be a mind reader, but politely ask, 'You seem to be feeling ... Is that right?' If they deny it, then accept their word for it. In this case, it might be worth checking your conscience – is this your stuff, your prejudices and assumptions? Are you trying to make more of this than is actually there? On the other hand, your ex may recognise and acknowledge that there is more to what they're saying than what is actually being said, and you may both be able to get a clearer understanding and move closer to a resolution.

When conversations go nowhere, it's nearly always because people aren't feeling listened to. Even if, ultimately, you disagree completely with what your ex is saying, make sure they know that you've heard. You might say something like, 'I hear that you would like to sell the house immediately and I understand that you're worried that you might soon be made redundant, but my position is that...' You may not reach a resolution, but hopefully you will both at least feel heard.

I'd like to offer you one final rule that will significantly increase the chances of communicating effectively with your ex: 'always give your ex the benefit of the doubt'. This applies whether you're communicating via text, email, telephone or face to face. Whether you're speaking or listening, always assume the best. This is not only for their sake, but also for yours. If they're agitated or impatient, maybe it's because they're stressed at work or feeling unwell, or just struggling with being separated and knowing how to talk. Don't jump to an instant conclusion that your ex is deliberately being difficult and trying to make your life hell. Keep persevering, being kind and courteous and sticking to your goal. If, after all your best efforts, good intentions and generous optimism, it becomes obvious that your ex is being obstructive, then it's time to move into conflict resolution mode (see Chapter 18).

Resolving Conflict

Unfortunately, it's not always possible to avoid an argument. Differences of opinion are inevitable between people so conflict will always be a part of life. However, there are things you can do to reduce the tension and speed up a resolution. There are also ways you can ensure that the battle isn't too bloody and doesn't leave permanent scars.

WHAT ARE YOU REALLY ARGUING ABOUT?

The first thing you need to know is what it is you're *really* arguing about. Many couples, together and separated, bicker and row for years without ever getting to the bottom of things. It can seem that the smallest of things can trigger you off, and emotions run high over the most trivial issues. When this is happening, even after you've separated and there's no relationship to fight for, then there is often something else going on under the surface. If you know that both of you are normally very reasonable and peaceful people, but you can never speak to each other without fireworks, then there's almost definitely a hidden payoff to your continued conflict.

ARGUING TO MAINTAIN CONTACT

For some couples it's simply about not wanting to let go. Arguing may be unpleasant, but all the time you have something that you can't agree on, you'll have to keep seeing each other, or at least maintain some sort of contact, in order to sort it out. Unconsciously, one or both of you feels that some contact, however negative, is better than no contact.

ARGUING TO MAINTAIN INTIMACY

It may be that you have to keep in contact with each other because of the children, or perhaps you work together or have some other sort of connection. So you still see each other regularly and you're able to be polite most of the time, but every now and again, something goes crazy and you have a massive row about something. In this case it could be that one or both of you is struggling to accept your relationship on its new level and you're missing the emotional connection you used to have. An argument may be the only opportunity you have to share your feelings with each other. While it may feel uncomfortable, it makes you closer, at least temporarily.

ARGUING TO MAINTAIN SELF-ESTEEM

Some couples continue to argue because they don't want to lose face. They feel that if they don't argue – perhaps on a particular issue or perhaps on any issue – then they are giving up and saying that the ex is right. Often the fear is that the ex is not only right about whatever the argument is about, but they're right in their views about them as a person and the breakdown of the relationship too. There is a sense that 'I have to prove that you are wrong and I am right'. It goes beyond right and wrong on external issues, and includes character and personality as well. So the argument is really about proving that you're an alright person and your ex is not.

ANGER

The other reason why many arguments develop and get out of hand is because our emotions get in the way. It is immensely frustrating when someone else can't understand something that, to us, is blindingly obvious. If we feel our rights are being violated or we're being unfairly treated, then the frustration can grow into justifiable anger. Unfortunately, whether it's justified or not, anger can cloud our judgement and make it harder for us to speak and listen effectively. When anger steps into the frame, often our goals step out. The argument becomes about our feelings rather than about the issue we're hoping to resolve.

In an argument, anger can take two very distinct paths, internal or external. When anger is externalised it might be expressed through shouting, interrupting, dragging up other issues, abusive language and physical gesturing. Consequently, it's easy to understand how this obvious display of anger can damage effective communication. The symptoms of internal anger – sighing, eye rolling, tutting, becoming monosyllabic or totally silent – can be equally destructive.

MANAGING YOUR ANGER

Whether your anger is internal or external, you need to control it when you get into conversation with your ex. Being prepared is one of the best ways of pre-empting anger. If you've rehearsed what you want to say and you've considered the reaction and your response, then you're much more likely to be able to stay rational. However, life often doesn't go to plan.

When you do begin to feel anger rising, the first thing to do is to acknowledge your feelings and slow yourself down. Recognise that you're getting angry and see if you can pinpoint why. If you can identify what's wound you up, you should address this issue first. For example, you may be feeling angry because you're not being understood, in which case you need to focus on how you can explain yourself better. If your anger is because your ex keeps changing the subject then politely say you really want to try and stick to the point.

All the time you're doing this you also need to be calming yourself down. In Step Two we looked at how our thoughts keep our emotions alive, and how, by changing our thoughts, our emotions will begin to subside. Therefore you need to be pouring bucket loads of positive thoughts over yourself. You need to reassure yourself that you're okay and that you can remain calm and focused. Be patient and take your time. The most important thing is to reach a mutually acceptable goal. You are in control of your feelings; you are not being controlled by the circumstances or your ex. Even if your ex is really annoying, you can still choose to maintain your equilibrium and your dignity and conserve your energy for seeking a solution.

If your anger tends to be internal, then you also need to keep reminding yourself to stay engaged. Watch your body language and continue to speak and listen respectfully. If you lean more towards outward anger, then you also need to make sure that your body language and verbal language are not intimidating in any way.

Anger is a physical as well as an emotional response, and reducing the physical sensations of anger will help you to calm down. You may find the following acronym – BRAGS – will help you to relax both physically and emotionally.

B = Breathing. Many people breathe more shallowly when they get angry, which exacerbates the physical response. Concentrate on long deep breaths to further relax muscles and slow down your central nervous system.

R = Relax. When we get angry we release adrenalin and our muscles begin to tighten up. Make yourself consciously relax your muscles, shake out clenched hands, shrug your shoulders and move your head from side to side to relieve neck muscles.

A = Awareness. Make sure you continue to be aware of what's going on around you and the bigger picture of your conversation and communication. When we get angry, we often get lost in the moment and lose awareness of what's most important.

G = Grounding. If you're not already sitting down, do so and concentrate on feeling the chair beneath your bottom and the floor beneath your feet.

S = Space. Make sure you give both of you sufficient physical space. For example, not too 'in their face' but also not sulking angrily behind folded arms and legs.

Another technique to slow down anger is to imagine that someone is watching you. That could be your mum, your children, your boss or Big Brother himself. It doesn't matter who it is as long as it's someone whose opinion you value, someone you wouldn't want to see you when you're out of control. Imagine that they are in the corner of the room listening to everything you say and do.

If none of this is working then the final tool in your kit bag is time out. If you can feel your anger continuing to rise and you can't do anything to reduce it, then stop the conversation – immediately. Apologise that your anger is getting in the way of talking, and explain that to continue to talk would be counterproductive. Then agree to contact your ex as soon as possible to arrange a mutually convenient time to continue. It may not be the ideal ending, and you probably won't have reached your goal, but at least you won't have made anything worse.

MANAGING YOUR EX'S ANGER

If your ex is the one that gets angry then the first thing to remember is that, now you're separated, their emotions are their business and their problem, not yours. You need to stay focused on ways to minimise their anger so you can get back on track to reaching your goal. It will probably feel very frustrating that you have to make allowances for their emotions and try to make it easier for them, especially if you feel they're doing nothing to help themselves. Remember, though, that you're doing this because you want to get things sorted out as quickly as possible. Learning to manage their anger better is for your benefit, not theirs.

> Violence or threats of violence are never okay. If conversations are always aggressive, or if you're avoiding resolving issues because you're scared of things getting out of control, then you should seek help at once. There are details of helping agencies at the back of this book.

Whenever possible, try to have conversations in a public place such as a pub or park to reduce the chance of your ex getting angry in the first place. If they do, the following ideas may help.

If you can notice their anger early enough, you may be able to stop it escalating. First, acknowledge that they're angry and make sure you continue to listen attentively. Show that you can continue to respect how they think and feel, and maintain your calm in spite of their emotions. If appropriate, try to be conciliatory. Demonstrate that you want to find a peaceful solution and work together in everyone's interests. Apologise if you need to and be gracious enough to admit it if you've been in the wrong. Also, be prepared to give an apology in part wherever possible. For example, you can be sorry that you've lost your job and can no longer afford the same financial agreement without backing down on what you're offering. Or you may be sorry that your ex is going to miss some of the old holiday photos but still maintain that it's fair that you have half.

Two other techniques that can diffuse an angry outburst are fogging and broken record. Fogging means taking the wind out of your opponent's sails by agreeing with them to some extent. For example, if you're accused of being unreasonable about contact arrangements, you could agree that sometimes you don't plan far enough ahead and you should make more effort. Or if the criticism is that you're being too slow in making decisions, you might agree that you have been very preoccupied with work recently. The broken record technique can be added to this to keep you heading towards your goals. Basically, it means firmly but continually going back to the point you want to make. For example, you might say, 'I understand that you're angry but we still need to...' or, 'I agree that I've not always made things easy for you, but we still need to...'

Finally, do remember that it's okay for you to share your feelings too. If you're angry or upset or feel intimidated by your ex's anger, say so. Let them know that you're not superhuman and you also struggle with difficult emotions. In spite of that, however, you want to resolve your issues so you both move on with your lives.

If your efforts are failing and your ex is getting angrier and angrier, then you may have no choice but to call a time out. When anger gets beyond a certain point, rational conversation goes completely out of the window. If your ex has lost their temper, then trying to continue a reasonable conversation is a waste of time. It will be much better to say you're sorry but you can't continue the conversation when they're like this, and you will contact them to rearrange another time when they're feeling calmer. Make sure you're not patronising as this will just fuel the fire further, but be polite and firm and walk away.

WHEN NOTHING'S WORKING

If you've hit a brick wall in communication with your ex but practical decisions for yourself and/or your children still need to be made, then you may decide to seek outside support. Your first port of call could be friends or family. If there are people around you whom both of you respect and care for, then perhaps they will be willing to act as a mediator for you. Do be aware, though, that you may be putting them in a very awkward position, and it may be difficult for them to be totally impartial. If this isn't appropriate, then you could consider professional mediation.

MEDIATION

Mediation aims to help you and your ex reach decisions that are fair for both of you without going through the courts. A trained mediator will help you both to focus on the practical issues you need to resolve relating to finances, property and your children's needs. Most people attend between two and six sessions, and at the end a written summary is produced which may be used by your solicitor to make an agreement legally binding if necessary.

For mediation to work, both you and your ex must be willing to attend sessions and be open and prepared to share the necessary information. Mediation can significantly help to reduce legal costs, but more importantly, it can reduce hostility, tension and misunderstandings.

Services vary around the country, but you can get a list of local mediators from the National Family Mediation Service or from your solicitor (see Further Help, page 203). If you've been through mediation and you still can't reach an agreement, or if your ex refuses to attend, then you may have no choice but to go through the legal system.

LEGAL INTERVENTION

If you haven't already done so, then you'll need to get yourself a solicitor. If you have children, choose a solicitor who's a member of Resolution, an organisation that ensures all work keeps the interests of children at the forefront. Resolution can also provide details of solicitors who practise Collaborative Family Law. Collaborative law is still fairly new, but basically it's a system where both you and your ex will appoint a solicitor, and the four of you will meet together to resolve your differences, rather than preparing cases and presenting them to a court. As well as avoiding court costs, this can also reduce legal fees for both of you as you are all working together with no hidden agendas. (For more on finding a solicitor, see Chapter 15.) Whatever the issue may be, your solicitor will advise you and help you to find the best way forward.

Unfortunately, there are some people who will not acknowledge and respect an agreement, even if it has gone through the court system. If this happens, you may be able to persuade your ex into mediation and re-negotiate the whole contract. For most, however, there's little choice but to go back to the courts. The reality is that often very little can be done. If your ex is still angry and bitter and single-mindedly refuses to play ball, you'll either have to wait it out or endure a lengthy legal battle with no guarantee of success.

COUNSELLING

Remember that whatever you're going through, you don't have to go through it alone. Relate counsellors are not there just for couples who want to stay together. You can see a counsellor on your own to get support or you can go as a separating couple. Relate counsellors are trained in helping couples who are divorcing to make sense of their emotions. You won't get the practical advice you can get from mediators, but they can help you with the listening and communicating techniques outlined earlier in the chapter, and enable you to focus on the task of getting over the brick wall.

Set Goals for the Future

Our final step on the journey is all about facing your future with curious confidence. We'll look at how being single can be a positive phase of your life when you have the chance to do many things you'd forgotten you wanted to do. We'll also look at the joys and hurdles of dating again before ending on the ultimate high of hopes, dreams and wild ambitions.

CHAPTER 19

Being Single and Being Satisfied

Congratulations – you're single. No, I'm not joking. You may not believe it right now, or you may have days when you seriously doubt it, but being single really can be a cause for celebration. You're free and independent. You can make decisions about how you spend your time and who you spend it with. Your life is yours to live how you choose.

You may have children and other family commitments and a job to take into account, but you have considerably more freedom and more choices than when you were with your ex. That's not to say that your ex was necessarily an unreasonable person who imprisoned you and refused to let you have a life of your own, but over the years you will have made numerous compromises and concessions to accommodate your differences. It's the way that relationships work and that's absolutely fine, but now you have the opportunity to reclaim the allowances you made.

It may have been many, many years since you were last single, and your new-found freedom and choices may feel more like a burden than an opportunity. Time can hang very heavy when you suddenly discover you've got more of it, and many people just don't know what to do with themselves without a partner around for company. Many people feel lost, but you can turn that around and see this as a phase in your life to be utilised for your benefit. You may not intend staying single for long, or you may think you'll be single for ever, but either way you can make this a time in your life that is both rewarding and satisfying. You can focus on yourself, on your needs and your desires; and discover, or rediscover, the many other ways that you like to spend your time, apart from with a partner.

RECLAIMING YOUR FREE TIME

When we're close to someone and spend a lot of time with them, a lot of our interests and friendships can begin to merge and we lose some of the things we used to enjoy. It's not conscious; it's just the way things often go as a relationship develops. Undoubtedly, you will have kept some of your own interests, but other things tend to fizzle out or lose their appeal because your partner doesn't share your enthusiasm. Sometimes it's a friendship that drifted apart because your partner didn't like them or you didn't feel able to take the time away from your relationship to keep the friendship alive. Or there may have been social activities that you always fancied having a go at that your partner pooh-poohed or didn't support in some other way. Now you only have yourself to please, and how you spend your spare time is completely up to you.

So, what have you stopped doing that you can now start again? What have you always fancied doing but never got round to? Take a look at the list below and see if it rings any old bells:

➤ Food – things you enjoyed cooking and eating that your ex didn't like

➤ Eating out – a particular restaurant or style of food: Italian, Thai, sushi

➤ Television programmes and film genres you used to love

➤ Computer games you've stopped playing or not had a chance to get into

➤ Books you'd like to read – novels, self-help books, biographies

➤ DIY or decorating jobs around the home

➤ Gardening ideas – landscaping and planting schemes

➤ Home exercise routines or meditative practices

➤ Personal development projects – overcoming a personal struggle or developing new strengths

➤ Further education – evening classes

➤ Sporting activities – individual, paired or team games

➤ Places you want to visit – towns, gardens, country homes, beauty spots

➤ Sports you'd like to follow, live or/and on television

➤ Leisure pursuits – walking, wine making, sailing, handicrafts, beekeeping

➤ Voluntary or community work

➤ Joining a social group – school, work, community, political or faith-based

➤ Friends you've lost touch with or see less than you'd like to

➤ Going to see new bands

➤ Listening to a particular genre of music

➤ Getting into online social networking

If this has sparked some ideas of things you'd like to take up again or try, then write them down as a goal. Remember the SPORT rule on page 92, and bear in mind that you may not be single for ever so make the timescale reasonably soon.

FRIENDSHIPS

Think again about how being single gives you the opportunity to deepen the friendships you have and develop new ones. You may have more time on your hands now than you'll ever have again so do make the most of it. If you haven't written any goals specifically relating to your friendships, then write some now. Who would you like to get to know better? Who do you want to see more often? Who do you want to get closer to? Would you like more friends to share certain things with? Do you want to find a tennis partner, another single mum, someone who shares your love of gardening? Would you like to get to know more people of the opposite sex, or more people who are in a different age group? Our lives are shaped by the company we keep, so what shape do you want your life to take in the future? It's up to you.

MAKING THE MOST OF WORK

The other area of our lives that can give us a lot of satisfaction is our work. That could be voluntary work, paid employment, part-time or full-time. You might work for yourself or as a full-time carer or parent. Whatever form your work takes, it is a place where you can feel good about what you give and produce and what you receive in terms of financial and/or emotional reward.

When you're in a relationship, your work often takes on a different meaning. You're no longer doing it just for your own benefit, but also for the two of you. You may have to earn a level of income that supports you both or contributes significantly to your joint budget. Or you may have to tailor your hours around the needs of your relationship, making sure you don't get so emotionally involved that you no longer have any energy to give your partner when you get home. Now you're single, however, it's all change. You probably still have to earn a living, but unless you have children to support, the standards you choose to live to are up to you alone. If you're a carer, then you'll still have commitments to uphold, but you can use any additional time to work towards something you might like to do in the future.

Being single can provide you with an excellent opportunity to focus on your work life, to commit more time and energy to it than you did before. Alternatively, it's a chance for you to take time out and do something completely different, to re-evaluate what you do and consider any changes you'd like to make. Would you like to retrain in a different field altogether or gain some new skills to enhance your current job? Would you like to take evening classes in a new field or are there training packages available where you work already? How about volunteering as a way of getting into another field or trying your hand at different things? You may be totally happy with how your work life is already, but if not, being single is a great opportunity to change it.

No one can tell how long they'll be single for. You may meet the new love of your life before you finish reading this book, or it may be a few years down the line. Or you may decide that being single is so satisfying that you don't want to be in another relationship. One thing that's for sure is that how you use the extra time that being single provides is totally up to you. You can be sad and pine for your couple days, or you can use it to grow your personal and professional life.

CHAPTER 20

Finding Love Again

'Once bitten, twice shy' – the famous saying expresses the way many divorced people feel about finding love again. If you've been hurt before then it's totally understandable that you might feel cautious and anxious about getting into another relationship. However, four out of 10 weddings in the UK are second marriages, which surely goes to prove that it is possible to meet someone special and fall in love again.

The timing is completely up to you. Some people find themselves being bowled off their feet when they least expect it; but on the whole, it's up to you to decide when you're ready to start looking for a relationship again. If your marriage had been terminal for some time and the ending was expected, then you may have done much of your mourning while you were still together; consequently you may be ready and open for someone new within a few months of separating. However, if your break-up was very sudden then it may take you some years before you're able to think about sharing your life with someone else. There's certainly no right or wrong time; only you can decide when you're ready. The following questions might help you to consider where you're at:

1. Are you able to understand and accept what went wrong in your marriage?
2. Are you able to look back at your marriage without feeling overwhelming sadness, anger, guilt, regret or resentment?

3. Are you comfortable with your own company and the occasional feelings of loneliness?
4. Do you enjoy meeting new people and finding out more about them?
5. Do you know what kind of person and what kind of relationship you're looking for?

If you can answer yes to all these questions then you're ready to consider dating. If you can answer yes to all of them except number five, then you need to do a bit more preparation but you're basically ready. If your answer was no to any of the first three, then you probably need more time before you can close the door on your past and step into your future.

GETTING READY FOR DATING

Before you throw yourself out there on the dating scene, you need to do a bit of preparation. Like many newly divorced people, you may be feeling like a fish out of water. Years may have passed since you last went on a date – or perhaps they called it 'courting' in your day.

First and foremost, you need to answer question five in the above list. Who and what are you looking for? Are you happy to meet someone who will be a potential life partner, or someone just for friendship and evenings out? Or are you looking for a sexual partner? Indeed, you may be looking for all of these or be happy to accept what you can find, but do be prepared for the fact that others on the dating scene may only be looking for one thing – sex or marriage.

Second, what kind of person are you looking for? What personality traits or experiences are most important to you? Must they look a certain way, have a particular job or hobby, be a parent or child-free? I'm sure we'd all like a Brad Pitt or

Angelina Jolie, but if we're honest, we know that someone in their league is unlikely to be looking for us. By all means set your sights high, but do be realistic and don't set yourself up to fail.

The next thing you might want to consider in your preparations is your level of self-confidence. How do you feel about your looks and your ability to 'pull'? Would you benefit from a bit of a makeover? Perhaps you need to spend a few more hours at the gym, get a new haircut and update your wardrobe. Ask a trusted friend what they think about the image you're projecting or, if you've got kids and you're brave enough, ask them. (If you need to work more on your general self-esteem, look back to Chapter 7.)

The final thing you need to do is make the decision that you are looking for a relationship. A few lucky people are able to meet someone when they're not looking, but the vast majority have to make a commitment to look. Nobody met someone else by staying at home and doing nothing. You're going to have to make a conscious decision to get yourself out there.

To prevent apathy and dating fatigue setting in, experts recommend that you schedule a break every now and again. So you might decide to hit the dating scene for four months and then take one off, or you might commit to a longer period of six to twelve months, and then take a couple of months off to review. Not only will these regular breaks give you the opportunity to take stock of how you're doing and recharge your batteries, but they will also help you remember that there is still much more to your life than looking for a partner.

WHERE TO LOOK

Research concludes over and over again that most people meet their marriage partner either through work or through friends, so these are the first places you should look. Think about joining any social clubs at work and getting involved in social activities. If friends invite you round for dinner or to a party, make sure you go. While there's no guarantee that you'll meet someone in these environments, if someone single is there you already have a lot of things in common to talk about.

If there's no one within your existing work or friendship environment, then look at your wider social networks. Think back to Chapter 12 where we looked at expanding your social life. All the areas you identified then are potential opportunities for meeting someone. So think about taking up a new sport, hobby or evening class – anything you're interested in where other people will be. You may not meet an actual partner there, but you may well meet their brother, mum or best friend.

Once you've got all those options up and running you might want to check out your local pubs and clubs. There will be certain places where singles are known to hang out, so you can be confident that you'll be in like-minded company. Lonely hearts ads in your local paper, online dating services, speed dating and other introduction agencies all provide excellent opportunities to meet other 'would like to meets'. They can be a bit daunting at first so, before getting involved, do some research. Find out more about the organisation, how long it's been running, what rules and selection criteria they use and, most importantly, what their success rates are.

HOW TO LOOK FOR A PARTNER

There isn't enough room in this book to begin to scratch the surface of all the ins and outs of dating, but here are a few ideas. The most important thing is to be yourself, and to be confident in being yourself. There are numerous tips and techniques to do with body language, eye contact and chat-up lines, but all of that advice has to fit within the context of you feeling comfortable within your own skin. There's absolutely no point going out there and pretending to be someone you're not. Not only will you feel increasingly uncomfortable as you try to keep up the façade, but your date will also wonder what on earth is going on and probably make a swift exit.

TOP DATING TIPS

1. **Be prepared.** Find out about your local area and get yourself physically, emotionally and psychologically ready to hit the dating scene. Make yourself feel good inside and out, and practise your flirting skills at every opportunity.

2. **Quantity does make a difference.** The more people you meet, the more chance there is that you'll meet someone you like and who likes you.

3. **Be yourself.** If you want someone to like you then you've got to be yourself. There's no point getting someone to fall for someone that you're not.

4. **Keep yourself safe.** Take sensible precautions. Make sure you don't give out your address or phone number online until you know someone really well, and always meet first dates in a public place and have a plan for how you'll get home.

5. **Be interested and interesting.** The art of conversation is actually easier than most people think. Be genuinely interested in them and finding out more about them, and be ready to talk about the things that are important to you. Do remember, though, not to turn a new date into a therapy session and start talking about your ex all night.

6. **Don't be too desperate.** No matter how much you think the person you've just met is the man/woman of your dreams, try to stay cool. Too much enthusiasm can come across as intimidating so relax and take your time.

7. **Be open-minded.** Don't jump to conclusions about people based on how they look or on the first few sentences that come out of their mouth. Unless they've said something that really offends you, try to get to know people before you rule them out.

8. **Learn to handle rejection.** Accept the fact that you are going to be turned down. You might never exchange numbers or get a second date, or you may see each other for a few weeks and then it'll be over. This is the reality of dating – try not to take it too personally.

9. **Enjoy yourself.** Dating should be fun. You'll probably meet lots of different people and go to many different places. If more comes out of it, great; but if not, at least you can have a good time.

10. **Don't give up.** It may take you a lot longer than you think to meet someone special so you're going to have to be patient. There are bound to be days when you feel despondent, and every now and again it's good to take a total break from the dating scene, but remind yourself regularly that good things come to those who wait.

CHAPTER 21

Hopes, Dreams and Wild Ambitions

Today is the beginning of the rest of your life. What do you want to do with it? Do you want the years to come to be better than the years you've left behind? Do you want your divorce to symbolise an ending or a new beginning?

No one denies that divorce is tough – indeed, it's probably one of the toughest things you'll ever experience – but it's also an opportunity to start afresh and do something new. We've already looked at changes you might want to make to your social life, in your friendship groups and at work; and we've looked briefly at how you might go about starting a new relationship if you're ready to. What about all the other stuff in life, though; perhaps things you've only ever dreamt of? Might this be an opportunity to explore and exploit some of these?

Below is just a taster of some of the areas you might like to explore.

TRAVEL

The world really is your oyster and now could be a great time to think about where you want to go. Are there far-flung corners of the world you'd like to visit or particular cities or places of beauty? Would you like to walk the Inca Trail, climb Kilimanjaro, swim with dolphins, see the Grand Canyon? Closer to home, are there European cities you'd like to see, or the vineyards of France, the German beer festival, the Swiss Alps? Let's not forget the UK – how about setting a challenge to visit every cathedral in the UK, drive every Roman road or drink a Costa in every market town?

RELOCATE

If visiting somewhere isn't enough, how about moving there? If you've got children then you won't want to move too far away from them, so it could just be a move into the local town or out into the countryside. If you don't have children and your career allows, you could move to a completely different part of the country, or join the millions of expats around the world and emigrate.

POLITICAL/SOCIAL ACTIVITY

Is there a political or social activist or supporter in you that's desperate to get out? Would you like to get more involved in a political party, either as a supporter or a candidate? Maybe you'd like to campaign on a social issue such as poverty, housing, immigration, children and young people's welfare, physical or mental health, the elderly, education or public services. There are charities that specialise in environmental projects, working in the Third World, seeking peace in conflict zones and fighting for international human rights. If something gets your blood boiling or pulls on your heart strings, why not find out how you can get involved to make a difference.

IMAGE CHANGE

As well as changing the world, you might want to do something radical to change yourself. Have you always fancied going blonde? Or growing a beard? Or getting into a completely different style of dress? Would you like to be much slimmer or investigate cosmetic surgery?

SPECIAL TREATS

There are many little extra purchases that we don't buy when we're with a partner. It can feel selfish to spend that money on yourself, especially if it's something that only you will enjoy. You may not be able to afford to go straight out and buy yourself the sports car you've always wanted, but you can start saving. Some treats are expensive; some not. A new car, boat or personalised number plate are at the top end, but lower down you might fancy treating yourself to a Gucci handbag, a Hugo Boss suit, a weekend at a spa, a new set of golf clubs or a Wii. Don't forget all the little things as well: a really nice bottle of bubble bath or single malt whisky, a computer game or regular subscription to your favourite magazine. Or perhaps a new sex toy for those quiet evenings alone!

SPIRITUALITY

For some, a massive upheaval like a divorce is a time when they reflect not just on matters of the head and heart, but also on those of the soul. You may never have thought about spirituality before, or it may be something you lost years ago. Perhaps you've often been curious to find out more but never quite knew where to start. Spirituality means many different things to people. You may simply want to find out more about the practices of certain religions, such as the Christian faith, Islam or Judaism, or perhaps you'd like to know more about Buddhist or shamanic practices. Why not start your own quest to find out what spiritual enlightenment could do for you?

On that lofty note, we reach the end of this chapter and the end of this book. We have explored so many things: the ups and downs and highs and lows of divorce; the ways it can limit some of your options but also how it can expand your opportunities in life. Perhaps an apt way of ending would be with the words of the famous serenity prayer, well known by many who've struggled, and continue to struggle, with life's many challenges:

> *God, grant me the serenity to accept the things I cannot change,*
> *The courage to change the things I can,*
> *And the wisdom to know the difference.*
>
> *Amen*

And Finally...

So here you are at the end of this book. Are you beginning to feel healthier or are you feeling a bit overwhelmed by the size of the mountain yet to climb? If it's the latter, please don't worry. As with all the major changes we go through in life, there'll be good days and bad days; times when you're filled with energy and optimism, and times when you want to give up and stay in bed with the duvet over your head.

Putting your life back together after divorce is a long and painful process for many, but hopefully it's one that you now feel more equipped to face. I hope you will strive for a life that's not just about surviving the break-up, but one that's also rich and rewarding.

This book may be over, but your journey has just begun. Inevitably, there will be twists and turns along the way, hills and valleys and perhaps a few endless plateaus, but take time to enjoy the journey and remember you're not alone. Millions have walked this way before you and many more are following behind. If you open your eyes, you're bound to find a few travelling companions along the way who are more than willing to share the views.

Further Help

HELPLINES

Relate – 0300 100 1234
National Mediation – 0845 60 30 809
National Domestic Violence – 0808 2000 247
Parentline Plus – 0808 800 222
National Debt Line – 0800 138 5445
Consumer Credit Counselling Service – 0800 138 111

BOOKS

Relate books, especially:
Help Your Children Cope with Your Divorce, Paula Hall
(Vermilion, 2007)
Loving Yourself, Loving Another, Julia Cole
(Vermilion, 2001)
Moving On, Suzie Hayman (Vermilion, 2001)
Step Families, Suzie Hayman (Vermilion, 2001)

Cognitive Behavioural Therapy for Dummies, Rob Willson
and Rhena Branch (John Wiley and Sons, 2005)
I Can Mend Your Broken Heart, Paul McKenna & Hugh
Willbourn (Bantam Press, 2006)
Managing Anger, Gael Lindenfield (Thorsons, 2000)
Self Esteem, Gael Lindenfield (Thorsons, 2000)

Teach Yourself Flirting, Sam Van Rood (Teach Yourself, 2006)
Thrifty Ways for Modern Days, Martin Lewis
(Vermilion, 2006)

WEBSITES

www.cccs.co.uk
The Consumer Credit Counselling Service is a charity that provides free debt and budgeting advice tailored to your situation.

www.clearstart.org
A national organisation that provides free support and help to people with serious debt problems.

www.collabfamilylaw.org.uk
An information site on family law.

www.directgov.gov.uk
A general public service site that provides legal information on separation and divorce.

www.divorceaid.co.uk
An independent group of professionals providing excellent all-round advice and support on every aspect of divorce and separation. Also provides resources for children and teenagers.

www.MIND.org.uk
The UK's national association for mental health.

www.moneymadeclear.fsa.gov.uk
The UK's financial watchdog, the FSA has a user-friendly website with a range of helpful information and booklets offering advice on financial matters.

www.nfm.org.uk
The website of National Family Mediation, a well-established and network of local Family Mediation Services.

www.parentlineplus.org.uk
A national charity with decades of experience in supporting parents and carers via a range of free, flexible, innovative services.

www.pinktherapy.com
The UK's largest independent therapy organisation working with gender and sexual minority clients.

www.relate.org.uk
Relate offers advice, relationship counselling, sex therapy, workshops, mediation, consultations and support, face to face, by phone and through their website.

www.resolution.org.uk (formerly known as The Solicitors Family Law Association)
An organisation of 5,000 family solicitors who are committed to resolving disputes in a non-confrontational manner.

www.respect.uk.net
Provides information and help for perpetrators of domestic violence.

www.TheRelationshipSpecialists.com
An independent website of trained, qualified counsellors providing online advice on any aspect of relationships, divorce, sexual problems and family issues.

www.womensaid.org.uk
A national domestic violence charity that provides support, advice and temporary accommodation to women and men affected by violence or abuse.

Index

207

assets list 130–1
calculate your equity 130–1
cash flow calculation 132–3
debts list 130–1
financial impacts of divorce 129
liquid assets 130, 131
monthly expenditure list 132–3
monthly income list 132–3
negative equity 130–1
personal resources or opportunities 133
financial responsibilities 30
financial settlement 130
first year after separation 159–60
'fit' of a relationship
changes in the fit 23–4
definition 20
recognising your original fit 20–3
unconscious fit 21–2
understanding the cause of breakdown 19
unspoken agreements 20–3
when the fit breaks 25–7
forgiving yourself for past mistakes 62–3
friends
effects of divorce 32, 117
ex-partner as a friend 113–14
ex-partner's friends 112–13
financial help from 133
impacts of your divorce 114–15
maintaining friendships 32
support from 101–4
friendship goals 188
friendship map 103–4
after divorce 118–19
friendships after divorce
deepening friendships 121–3
expanding your friendships 123–5
friendship map 118–19
how you would like your friendships to be 118–19
nurturing friendships 119–21
re-evaluating 32, 117
your intimacy circle 118–19
future hopes, feelings of loss 39
future plans and ambitions
image change 198–9
political activity 198
relocation 198
social activism 198
special treats 199
spirituality 199–200

travel 197–8
see also dating

goal-setting action plan 92–5
goals for the future see dating; future plans and ambitions
grandparents 32
grief
action plan 86–7
and fear 39, 44–7
considering things that you won't miss 43–4
feelings of loss 39–40
suggestions to help the grief process 41–5
when it turns to depression 41
why some cope better than others 40–1
guilt 59
action plan 88–9
forgiving yourself 62–3

happiness, media myths about 44
health, taking responsibility for 31
hobbies, developing new interests 33
holidays 159
home
financial pressure to sell 131
loss of a secure base 79
making a new home for yourself 30
missing having someone around 76–7
missing your home 79
need for home comforts 79
safe and comfortable home for the children 30
housing, practical challenges 138–9

identity, feelings of loss 39
image change, future plans and ambitions 198–9
income, monthly income list 132–3
inner voice
changing the message 85, 87, 89–90
effects on our self-esteem 67–8
instant chat on the Internet 120–1
intellectualisation as defence mechanism 11–12
Internet, nurturing friendships 120–1
intimacy circles 103–4, 118–19
isolation 81, 82
action plan 89–90

210

Also available from Vermilion:

relate

Help Your
Children Cope
with Your
Divorce

Paula Hall

When parents decide to separate, their children's lives are changed forever. This sensitive, accessible guide includes clear advice and guidance on how to minimise the impact on your children.

Acknowledging the personal difficulties faced by the adult who has made the decision to leave, as well as the adult who has been left, this book is for all parents going through a divorce or separation who are concerned for their children.

relate
STARTING
AGAIN
HOW TO LEARN FROM THE PAST FOR A BETTER FUTURE

Sarah Litvinoff

When a relationship finishes it can feel like the end of the world, but it is also a new beginning. In *Starting Again*, Sarah Litvinoff looks at the lessons that can be learnt from a relationship that has ended and helps you to deal with your feelings of separation, grief and recovery.

Through self-assessment questionnaires, tasks and discussion points, you will reach a greater understanding of yourself and your relationships and be able to start looking to a positive future. This book will help you to come to terms with the ending of a relationship and assess what went wrong, become aware of and break patterns you have unconsciously repeated, start again and build a new social life for yourself.

In *Moving On*, Suzie Hayman draws on her many years of experience as a Relate counsellor and agony aunt and provides information, advice and practical strategies to help you cope, as positively as possible, with the stress of breaking up with your partner. You will learn how to manage negative feelings, help your children through the difficult process, communicate with your partner and children throughout, cope with shared parenting responsibilities and sort out financial issues.

Sympathetic, sound and full of positive, practical advice, this is an invaluable guide for all those facing the breakdown of their relationship.

☐ **Help Your Children Cope**
with Your Divorce   9780091912833   £8.99

☐ **Moving On**   9780091856250   £9.99

☐ **Starting Again**   9780091856670   £7.99

FREE POSTAGE AND PACKING
Overseas customers allow £2.00 per paperback

ORDER:

By phone: 01624 677237

By post: Random House Books
c/o Bookpost
PO Box 29
Douglas
Isle of Man IM991BQ

By fax: 01624 670923

By email: bookshop@enterprise.net

Cheques (payable to Bookpost) and credit cards accepted

Prices and availability subject to change without notice.
Allow 28 days for delivery.
When placing your order, please mention if you do not wish
to receive any additional information.

www.rbooks.co.uk